GERMANY *vs.* CIVILIZATION
NOTES ON THE ATROCIOUS WAR

GERMANY *vs.* CIVILIZATION

NOTES ON THE ATROCIOUS WAR

BY

WILLIAM ROSCOE THAYER

And he will be a wild man; his hand will be against every man, and every man's hand against him.

Genesis XVI, 12.

BOSTON AND NEW YORK

HOUGHTON MIFFLIN COMPANY

The Riverside Press Cambridge

1916

Published March 1916

NOTE

WHILE this book is on the press, President Wilson has taken a firm stand, from which, we may hope, he will put an end to foreign arrogance and to domestic plotting and sedition. My references to his policy, written earlier, reflect the grave anxiety which many of us felt during the autumn and winter, and I let them remain because they bear witness to a very important element in the crisis. The long period of doubt over the President's intentions not only stifled American patriotism, but greatly encouraged the enemies at work in the United States.

In this sketch I have purposely assembled a sufficient body of the characteristic doctrines of the shapers of Prussian policy, from Frederick the Great to General Bernhardi, to remind the reader of the essential German elements underlying the Atrocious War. These will enable him to see that my own conclusions are based on German premises and facts, and not on calumnies invented by foreigners. During the progress of the struggle, such essentials are often forgotten, or are obscured by excitement over military, naval, or diplomatic events. Nothing is more important, however, than that the origins of this conflict, and the doom which awaits Civilization unless Kultur is crushed, be thoroughly understood.

W. R. T.

CAMBRIDGE, MASSACHUSETTS
March 6, 1916.

CONTENTS

GERMANY *vs.* CIVILIZATION

CHAPTER I

HUMILIATION — NOT THANKSGIVING

> O, well for him whose will is strong.
> He suffers, but he will not suffer long;
> He suffers, but he cannot suffer wrong.
> TENNYSON.

FOR the second time since the Atrocious War began, the President of the United States calls upon us Americans to observe a day of Thanksgiving, on which we shall express gratitude for the manifold blessings Providence has showered upon us.

Our harvests have surpassed all bounds. Our industries, under the unhealthy stimulus of war, have raised the wages of millions of laborers. Like the Pharisee we can thank God that we are not like our neighbors: they are at war, we are at peace.

A year ago, President Wilson bade us hold a similar Thanksgiving; and those who have the catchwords of religion on their lips, but infidelity in their hearts, might infer — from our increased prosperity — that our prayers and thank-offerings were acceptable, and have been rewarded in overflowing measure.

But those are not gods of the spirit who substitute gifts of corn and copper and iron and gasolene for the spiritual gifts, for lack of which our souls perish. In this crisis a true prophet of the soul would call us not to thanksgiving but to humiliation — the humiliation that every heart, into which the faintest instinct of nobleness has glimmered, must feel when it recognizes that it has betrayed the very law of its being.

During fourteen months the memory of our dark shortcoming, of our great refusal, has lain like a mildew on our American conscience. Some of us, singly, have repudiated the shame; but even if every American had made his private disavowal, we should not have been freed from our supreme obligation. It was for the President of the United States, sitting in the chair where Washington and Lincoln have sat, the guardian for the time being of the principles on which this Republic was founded, — the principles which have upheld it for one hundred and forty years, the principles which alone justify its existence and its perpetuation, — it was for President Wilson, speaking for this nation, to utter the word of repudiation which could have absolved us from the guilt of allowing Belgium to be violated without our protest.

He kept silent.

Day after day brought news of fresh atrocities committed by the Germans in Belgium. What might have been regarded at first as a few sporadic cases of such cruelty as often accompanies war, proved to be in truth only the beginning of the enforcement of a system of Frightfulness, deliberately planned years before in the Bureau of the Prussian General Staff, unhesitatingly approved by the German Emperor, and now carried out with diabolical precision. Very soon the weight of testimony became overwhelming, but. still President Wilson was silent. Considerations of policy, doubts as to expediency, flitted between him and his conscience. Perhaps the reported abominations were not true; it was the duty of the President of the United States to suspend judgment until he had heard all the evidence from every side; if he protested against the German acts, he would be accused of denying the neutrality which he had officially set up to guide this country throughout the War; the etiquette of diplomacy would regard such a protest as not only out of order, but as unmannerly; worse still, a moral protest not backed up by physical force would be futile, — as if a moral act could ever be futile, — and the Germans, who had announced that they took no heed of anything except physical force, would laugh at us.

And so President Wilson was silent.

The days slipped by and grew into weeks. Thousands of non-combatants, men, women, and children, died in agony. Even the inani-

mate objects of beauty, created by generations of men to whom the very name Prussian was happily unknown, and spared by
the ravages of countless earlier wars, were
wantonly destroyed.

The University of Louvain, with its gem-
like Library, was demolished; the Cathedral
at Malines sank in ruins; the masterpieces at
Ypres, at Arras, and at a score of other cities
went down; and when the devastators spread
into France, they made the Cathedral of
Rheims — the national shrine of French worship for seven hundred years — the target
of their artillery.

Still President Wilson was silent.

But while time brings opportunity it does
not take away remorse for opportunity neg-
lected. We sin in time, but our guilt cannot
be measured in terms of years: for sin and
remorse are moral not temporal.

Wherein lay our guilt? It lay in our failure
as a nation through the silence of the President to bear witness to the deepest truth

which civilized men have felt or can feel. A horde of military barbarians violated the neutrality of little Belgium, which we, with other governments, had pledged ourselves to uphold, — and we said nothing. And then that horde sped on, its gray-clad regiments sifting over Belgium, as the showers of ashes from Vesuvius once fell upon Pompeii with irremediable havoc. In this outrage on Humanity also, the Huns flung their challenge at us, and we said nothing.

But we of all the nations of the earth were bound by the strongest obligations to speak up for the sacred principles of humanity. We were the most powerful free people in the world, and to possess power imposes the obligation to use it in behalf of the weak. The little countries looked to us for leadership, looked and listened and waited, and we gave them neither sign nor sound. They would have joined us in protest even at the risk of bringing on themselves the fury of the Germans, within whose reach they dwelt. Our

silence — the silence of President Wilson —
"Letting 'I dare not' wait upon 'I would'" —
brought to them the desolating conviction
that the United States would officially utter
no declaration in behalf either of neutrality
or of humanity. We tacitly admitted that a
small nation has no rights, that neutral nations may be overrun and destroyed at the
pleasure of a powerful aggressor. The President's silence was tantamount to acquiescing
in the German doctrine that might is right,
that matter and not spirit rules the universe,
including the conduct and the affairs of men.
This is the primal infidelity.

So to our shame we let it be implied that
the Government of the United States was not
officially concerned in protesting against the
subversion of neutral rights, or the swallow-
ing up of a small nation by a large, or by
crimes against common humanity. It was as
if President Wilson, clothed with the moral
strength of the United States, had been walk-
ing on the bank of a stream, and had seen on

the other bank a colossal brute beating a little girl; and the President had said to himself: "There is no boat for me to cross by, and if I shout, the ruffian will only laugh. After all, my eyesight is not very good; perhaps I don't see clearly what he is doing. I ought not to protest unless I could verify the fact for myself; that is impossible; so I will look the other way and walk on."

Into such an abyss does consideration for the etiquette of diplomacy plunge those who set it above morals. In this aspect, diplomacy is indeed a code distilled from the immemorial experience of the guile and cruelty of rulers, which sanctions them in committing, as officials, crimes which all but the wickedest of them would shrink from as individuals. If plain Professor Woodrow Wilson had witnessed such an assault, we may be sure that he would not have doubted the veracity of his eyes, and that, though he had been unable to rescue the little girl from her assailant, he would have protested in loudest tones.

The assumption that nations and their rulers cannot be bound by the moral laws which bind individuals will not go on forever polluting the world. It also is the spawn of infidelity, and proceeds from the theory that men collectively — whether nations, hierarchies, parties, or corporations — are impersonal, abstract, and that, having no souls, they are shut out from moral concerns.

The diplomacy which seals the lips of the spokesman of a mighty nation, when he beholds a monster invade, outrage, torture, and destroy a tiny nation, is born of the Devil. It stifles chivalry; it leashes in the desire which is an instinct in the heart of every one worthy of the name of man to rush to the aid of the helpless in their distress; it strangles our common heritage of humanity, and substitutes for it a policy of selfishness, which evades responsibility for the fate of our fellow men. After Cain slew Abel, the Lord said unto Cain, "Where is Abel thy brother?" And he said, "I know not: Am I my brother's keeper?"

' So ancient and of such bad eminence is the precedent which tied the official tongue of the United States when the German Cain slew Belgium! The conscience of our countrymen sent its inquiry to Washington, "Where is Belgium?" and the silence at the White House mutely echoed Cain's reply, "I know not: Am I my brother's keeper?"

CHAPTER II

REALITY OR MIRAGE?

If we could only alter the Germans after the model of the English, if we could only have less philosophy and more power of action, less theory and more practice, we might obtain a good share of redemption, without waiting for the personal majesty of a second Christ.

ECKERMANN, *Conversations with Goethe.* March 12, 1828. [Bohn Translation, p. 319.]

BEFORE I proceed to trace the stages by which the ancient pagan ideals revived in Prussia, and how Prussia then diffused them — a moral Prussic acid — through Germany, I wish to recall that other Germany which many men and women not yet past middle age remember with affection and now with the regret born of a tragic disillusion.

Throughout the nineteenth century Germany was one of the chief fountains from which the English-speaking world drew most largely its supplies of philosophy and erudition; and of poetry, too, because the poetry of

Germany's Golden Age, produced by Lessing, Goethe, and Schiller, and by half a dozen balladists and lyric singers, came like a revelation, or new message, from Apollo to his devotees beyond the Alps and the Rhine and the Atlantic.

Coleridge, if not the earliest, was the first far-carrying voice to interpret German thought, and especially German philosophy, in England; but it was Carlyle, the mightiest of modern British advocates — persistent, indomitable, dynamic, uncompromisingly computing all deeds in terms of righteousness, with a fund of indignation and of humor unmatched among the Germans whom he introduced to English readers — Carlyle it was who raised a marvelous shrine to Goethe and to German ideals. It is hardly too much to say that for a considerable time Goethe was as the sun by which many persons lived their lives by day, and Kant was the moon by which they moved among the ultimate mysteries which enshroud man as by night. The springs of

Poesy became intermittent and then dry —
Heine, the latest, limpid, sparkling, swift,
ironical, melodious. But Philosophy flowed in
ever-swelling streams — Hegel, whose intoxi-
cating draughts caused his disciples to see
equivalence in things good and bad, black
and white, life and death, interchangeable
and therefore the same; and then Fichte and
Schelling and Schleiermacher; then darker and
darker streams, till we reach the inky pool of
Schopenhauer. Let the waters be what they
might, however, the thirsty world drank of
them eagerly, and it came to think of Germany as the land whose people were so ab-
sorbed in philosophizing about where man
came from and whither he was going, that they
paid little heed to his actual present state.

Erudition also kept even pace at first with
Philosophy, and then distanced it, and included it among the topics of erudite research.
While the Germans discovered few first principles, they were most nimble in seizing foreign
discoveries and in elaborating these through

every variation. They organized, if they did
not invent, a method of education, using that
word in its broadest sense, by which they re-
duced learning to a system as admirably classified as the best book of reference. In dealing
with ideas, they usually became doctrinaires;
in each German brain one idea and only one
grew at a time, like the plant or flower in a pot.
This promoted that single-mindedness which
lies behind German thoroughness. It has its
defects, of course; one sometimes is bored by
doctrinaire companions; it leads to Philistin-
ism — "The Germans," said Goethe, "cannot
cease to be Philistines"; [1] and there is always
the danger that if the same bad idea be planted
in the brains of nearly all the people of a one-
ideaed race, there will be uncurbed unanimity
for evil when the idea is translated into action.
Man and the Devil were joint occupants of the
first garden, and the Devil has not yet lost his
cunning as a horticulturist. Nevertheless, in
dealing with facts, particularly with the facts

[1] Eckermann, *Conversations*, p. 353.

of physics, chemistry, and philology, the erudite Germans made objectivity their standard, and strove to depersonalize themselves so
completely that the faculty by which they
observed might actually see the *Ding an sich*,
— the thing in itself, — beyond the idea of it
which alone enters human consciousness.

Foreigners sought the learning which the
German universities gave, and they went in
such increasing numbers, that from the last
quarter of the century onward they literally
swarmed at the chief institutions; and as these
students were unusually hungry for knowledge, they devoured avidly what was offered
them, becoming enthusiastic disciples of the
German method and of the professors who
taught it. Quite naturally, they looked back
with affection upon the German environment
amid which was planted their particular Tree
of Knowledge. Note however, that until after
1870 the universities they most frequented
were non-Prussian: so the Germans with
whom they came into friendly relations were

not Prussians, but Saxons and Rhinelanders, Suabians and Bavarians.

Among these, far into the century, life seemed easy-going. Each State had its army and its police and its punctilio, but they had not yet been standardized to the rigid machine-like pattern of Prussia. Indeed, the other Germans still dared to regard Prussia as the more cultivated Greeks used to regard Macedonia, and they openly ridiculed Berlin and the Berliners. Little cities like Düsseldorf and Stuttgart, large cities like Dresden and Munich, cultivated the arts. There was good music everywhere, and even small towns maintained a theatre where not only the classic German dramas, but also translations of Shakespeare and Molière were produced.

The traveler from England or America found much to amuse him in the German beds and mysterious bedclothes; in the cooking, with its inexhaustible supply of ham, sausage, and sauerkraut; in the beer gardens, where the girth of the habitués swelled visibly, as they

poured down quart after quart of black or
yellow beer: in the way in which men kissed
each other on every occasion, and in their
pompous taking off of hats and "having the
honor" whenever they met. The foreigner
noted also their porcelain stoves, on whose
hospitable tops babies were kept from freezing
on coldest nights, and the table manners, from
which he inferred that it was easier for a
learned German to discover a new asteroid or
a new chemical element, than the use of a fork.
In these and a hundred other superficial dif-
ferences, not to mention the amazing cos-
tumes, the foreigner's sense of humor was
constantly stirred.

But more serious aspects checkered his
amusement. He wondered, especially if he
came from America, at the extent to which
German men had shifted the heavy burdens
upon women. If he took a very early start, he
saw from the window of his carriage the peasant women trudging out with great baskets
on their backs to their work in the fields; and

at twilight he saw them trudging home, bent under the loaded baskets — while the men, carrying only a mattock or a scythe, smoking their porcelain-bowled pipes, plodded leisurely behind them. When he reached his *pension* he was startled — and at first he probably blushed — to see his heavy trunk loaded on the back of a housemaid, who carried it up three or four flights of stairs to his room. And so he never became quite accustomed to the sight of a woman and dog harnessed together, drawing a cart of milk cans and stopping from house to house, while the husband delivered the milk to his customers. "We have never taken quite the same view of women that you Americans do," Bismarck said to an American.

But after all, the traveler of three- or four-score years ago generally accepted the unpleasant or distressing conditions in a foreign country as part of the landscape for which he was not responsible; and his impression of Germany, as he saw it on the surface, was of a widespread, stolid contentment and of a sort of bovine comfort. The literacy of the common people surprised him; as well it might, for his bootblack had studied Greek and his cabby read Hegel, and even the peasant swains and lassies quoted Heine's love lyrics at each other: at least, he heard such statements from the intellectuals with whom he associated. The intellectuals themselves not merely enjoyed music — it was as indispensable to their daily life as books were. Every one in the family sang or played, and to attend concerts and the opera was not a luxury, to be indulged in sparingly, but a necessary, to be taken as regularly as one's food.

Foreign students, when they went home, bearing their doctors' diplomas like Olympic garlands, were the most enthusiastic praisers of German life. They forgot the unrestrained drinking and open dissoluteness which every student was expected to indulge in; but they remembered with gratitude their great obligations to their professors and the kindness of the professors' families; perhaps, also, their flirtations with flaxen-haired Dorotheas. Maturer observers described the Germans as a rather slow, heavy people, industrious, not disguising their self-esteem, taking all subjects (humor included) with scientific seriousness, sentimental, romantic and doctrinaire. And since their manners were crude, it was assumed that the Germans must be honest; it being a popular fallacy of long standing everywhere that rustic uncouthness and ignorance of the ways of the world bespeak native innocence and virtue. So, by an amusing twist of induction, bad manners or none are accepted as outward signs of inward grace.

The non-Prussians did not appear war-loving: on the contrary, while each State kept up an army, this seemed less with a view to make war than to provide an imposing display at parades and public ceremonies, and to give the nobles something to do. The little town of Weimar filled a much larger space in the thoughts and enthusiasm of those Germans than did the entire great Kingdom of Prussia;

and although Weimar had become only a whispering gallery for memories of Goethe and Schiller and their friends, it was the Mecca to which Germans and foreigners made their pilgrimage. And other quiet towns — Jena, Göttingen, Heidelberg, Bonn — enjoyed a reputation for intellectual leadership in comparison with which militarist pride still seemed second rate, if not vulgar. Down beyond 1870, the Germans placed Goethe far above Frederick the Great as the exponent of the highest German ideals.

The outside world thought of the non-Prussians, therefore, not as a race of fighters, but of thinkers, scholars, visionaries, fed on pigmeat and beer, careful tradesmen, docile peasants, and masterful musicians. So conspicuous was the visionary trait in them that until the middle of the century the Germans regarded themselves as irresolute. "Is Germany Hamlet?" — a question asked by one of their popular writers in the forties — was repeated and seriously discussed. Had excess of thought para-

lyzed the will to act? The political ineptitude
of the non-Prussian States seemed to spring
from an enfeebled will; and those States, after
submitting with comparatively little resentment to the hegemony of Austria, passed with
mixed emotions under the control of Prussia.
Not until the Prussian will energized them did
the non-Prussian Germans loom up as Moloch
worshipers, thirsting for world-empire.

I wish to seek the sources of that meta-
morphosis; to discover how far it was due to
the imposing of the vastly more dynamic Prussian will on the German, and how far to the
calling back to life of certain atavistic passions
common to the ancestors of Teutonic stock.
When a middle-aged man, burly and gruff but
at heart not cruel, who has led outwardly a
rather commonplace yet respected life, and
has shown marked talents for several high
objects, suddenly professes fiendish principles
and proceeds to carry them out with a deliri-
ous enjoyment, we turn to his family record
for earlier maniacal outbursts. Alienists, no

longer believing that Cains develop in the twinkling of an eye, consult heredity. Who can set a limit to the longevity of atavism? Seeds of corn taken from an Egyptian tomb, and planted now, germinate after four thousand years: may it be that ferocious instincts, which flourished in savage forerunners, can revive and overcome their descendants after the lapse of many generations?

The reader may cherish a still more glowing recollection of Germany than this which I have outlined; if he does — and he may well find reasons for it — he will feel with increased amazement the dark contrast between past and present.

CHAPTER III

ATAVISM

"From these old-German gloomy times," said Goethe, "we can obtain as little as from the Servian songs, and similar barbaric popular poetry. We can read it and be interested about it for a while, but merely to cast it aside, and let it lie behind us. Generally speaking, a man is quite sufficiently saddened by his own passions and destiny, and need not make himself more so by the darkness of a barbaric past. He needs enlightening and cheering influences, and should therefore turn to those eras in art and literature during which remarkable men obtained perfect culture, so that they were satisfied with themselves, and able to impart to others the blessings of their culture."

ECKERMANN, *Conversations*, October 3, 1828, p. 327.

WHAT of the German Cain who suddenly arose at the opening of the twentieth century, gigantic, merciless, mad with the purpose of slaying the small and feeble, of subduing the powerful whose spoils he coveted, of shattering the civilization which embodies the cumulative ideals of three thousand years, and of setting up his own civilization in its stead?

The Goths and Vandals and Huns who peopled Germany early in the Christian era, were as unqualified Barbarians as Apache Indians. They had an insatiable appetite for war; and this was whetted when they came into conflict with the Romans, because by war alone could they defend themselves and then make their inroads into the crumbling Roman Empire and secure its wealth. Even after they gained the mastery and had mixed their blood freely with that of the decadent peoples which Rome once swayed, they kept to an extraordinary degree the traits which dominated their ancestors when history first describes them. One of those traits, blood-thirstiness, crops out at intervals during all their subsequent annals, as surely as periodic dipsomania recurs to madden its victim. The beheading by Charlemagne of a multitude of Saxons at Verden was one manifestation of it; internecine war, accompanied by incredible horrors and prolonged during thirty years, was another; the devastation of Belgium and of Northeastern

France in 1914 was the latest. At the smell of blood, the *Furor Teutonicus*, proverbial for its wildness, has always been kindled.

Among the German Barbarians a spirit of vassalage also appears in the earliest accounts we have of them. "The chief fights for victory," says Tacitus; "his vassals fight for their chief. If their native state sinks into the sloth of prolonged peace and repose, many of its noble youths voluntarily seek those tribes which are waging some war: both because inaction is odious to their race, and because they win renown more readily in the midst of peril, and cannot maintain a numerous following except by violence and war. . . . Nor are they as easily persuaded to plough the earth and to wait for a year's produce, as to challenge an enemy and earn the honor of wounds. Nay, they actually think it tame and stupid to acquire by the sweat of toil what they might win by their blood." [1]

[1] Tacitus, *Germania*, chap. xiv (Church and Brodribb's translation).

Far from resenting vassalage, the Germans rejoiced in it: and in due time this spirit developed into Feudalism, the highest political conception which the Teutons have yet been able to devise. Elaborated a thousand years ago, it expressed so clearly, so frankly, so completely the Teutonic ideal, that in spite of changing outward conditions, it reappears to-day, under different name and outward disguise, as the utmost aim of the Germans.

Feudalism classified society into layers as rigidly as the steps of a pyramid rise from the base to the apex: at the bottom, slaves and serfs; at the top, the monarch. Except at the two extremes, the occupants of each layer not only looked up to those above them, but looked down on those beneath; and the satisfaction of looking down more than compensated for the irksomeness of looking up. The only liberty the German really coveted was the liberty of being and doing on his social plane just what every other dweller on that plane was and did. The habit of looking up intensified his innate submissiveness — a submissiveness expressed in Feudal terms by the loyalty of man to master, of vassal to lord. When he came to regard the monarch, it was with a reverence, unreasoning and absolute, which worshipers in other lands reserved for the Deity.

As the control of the monarch slackened, until it became hardly more than a political theory, the power of his chief vassals increased and they in turn aspired to be absolute monarchs in their several spheres, — princes, dukes, marquises, counts, — each holding tenaciously his independence, and each receiving from his subjects the worship they had once paid to the supreme sovereign. Germany was split up into many states, large and small, whose quarrels, whose striving for predominance, whose dynastic rivalries comprise an unedifying history for several centuries. We cannot understand the German Reformation itself if we look upon it simply as the effort of a new religion to supplant an old one: we must 'know how far political or family ambition caused each German ruler to cling to the old or to espouse the new.

Throughout this long evolution from Roman to recent times, amid all changes, the two traits which I have called blood-thirstiness and submissiveness persisted. Wherever the Germans fought, they fought with a savage relish of fighting, and they never lost the instinct which made them accept docilely orders from above. Slow, stolid, patient, persevering, they plodded on. Even as late as the eighteenth century they seemed almost to stagnate; no effective, unifying control bound the Pumpernickel States together; and as the princelings lacked initiative, their subjects could not supply it. In civilization, so far as this expresses itself in manners and in social conduct, the Germans were centuries behind their neighbors in Western Europe. Manners, indeed, seem always to have been beyond their reach; whether from a native obtuseness, which renders them dull to the charm of courtesy and high breeding, or from deliberate Chauvinism, which holds that, as bad manners are German and good manners are foreign, it would be unpatriotic and an admission of inferiority, to replace the indigenous product by an exotic.

Now arose, however, a leader in Germany. The House of Hohenzollern, sprung from medieval highwaymen, — their name suggests high-toll-taking gentry, — had come down from the mountains of South Germany and acquired, by successive marriages or conquests, possessions in the Rhineland and the Margravate of Brandenburg. In due time the Elector of Brandenburg created himself King of Prussia, the least civilized of all the German States. But those men of the Northeast, sprung from Slavic, Teutonic, and it may be in part from remote Asiatic strains, kept the traits which had made their predecessors formidable when the Christian era was young: and when one of the most masterful of modern despots awakened and drilled and led them, they responded with the wild joy possible only

to those who revert, after ages of disuse, to
their atavistic propensities.

Frederick the Great taught not only the
Prussians, but all other Germans, that the
strength and very existence of a nation such
as he planned depend upon its Army. Virtue,
literature, art, science, invention, industry, are
subordinate; the Army is indispensable, supreme. "Righteousness," said Solomon, "ex-
alteth a nation." The only exaltation which
Frederick relied upon or preached was that
of military Might. Frederick had no scruples,
and being backed by a sufficient force of Pomeranian grenadiers, he did not need them. He
was perfidious, he robbed, he persecuted, he
lied; but as his Army was stronger than that
of his adversaries he prospered. He laughed
at the suggestion that the Divine Vengeance
would repay the wicked. Had he not stolen
Silesia? Had he not joined in vivisecting Poland? If Divine Vengeance slept on while
he was perpetrating such crimes, it must be
either a myth or a nonentity; and as Frederick

respected realities only, an absentee avenger, or a God whose traces were only dimly discoverable in the Old Testament, had no terrors for him.

The Hohenzollerns who succeeded Frederick were brutish, but this would not have mattered if they had been competent. The Prussian Army deteriorated. Napoleon humbled Germany and stamped on its map the names of three great French victories, Jena, Eylau and Friedland. Then came the uprising, when at Leipsic the Germans, assisted by the Russians, Austrians, Bavarians, Swedes, and British, broke Napoleon's power. After Waterloo, they enjoyed again independence from foreign dictation, dearer to them than internal liberty. And yet the seeds of Liberty which the French Republic sowed throughout Europe sprang up during the next decades and they burst into brief flowering, in the revolution of 1848–49. Even in Prussia, the masses rose to secure constitutional freedom, and frightened Prince William into an ignominious flight. Presently

Reaction triumphed: the Liberals were defeated; their leaders either fled to America or were shot; the very name of Liberty was silenced.

And now a Prussian greater than Frederick rose up to steady Prussia's shaky nerves, to make Prussia mistress of Germany and Germany arbitress of Europe. To these ends Bismarck revived the Army as the necessary material weapon; but he relied also upon Diplomacy, which he practiced with no more scruples than Machiavelli taught his Prince to observe. By guile he trumped up a pretext for dismembering Denmark; by craft he inveigled Austria to join in that crime; by cunning he then forced Austria to fight for their common spoil; by the falsified Ems dispatch he infuriated France into declaring the war on Prussia which he had been secretly instigating for years. These were the methods by which he created the German Empire: this was the imperious statesman whom the Germans revere. Fit is it that the Prussian ideal should have

been embodied in Frederick the Great and in
Bismarck — men whose genius would have
had no play unless the millions of Germans
whom they mastered had been living on a
moral level where such methods were accepted
as ideal.

Over against Frederick and Bismarck let us
set two incarnations of American ideals, —
George Washington, the contemporary of
Frederick, and Abraham Lincoln, the contemporary of Bismarck. They, too, wrought
to create a nation and to preserve and unify it
— but their work was modern; their principle
was Liberty; their methods were moral and
humane: whereas Frederick might have been
the twin of Gaiseric, the Vandal, and Bismarck, the brother of Brennus, the Gaul.
"*Vae victis!*" "Woe to the conquered!"
Brennus shouted as he threw his sword into
the scales on which, in B.C. 389, the Romans
were heaping their ransom. "*Vae victis!*" was
Bismarck's motto, when he extorted his in-
demnity from strangled France in A.D. 1871.

Twenty-three centuries separated Brennus from Bismarck, but the Prussian ideal had not advanced beyond that of the Barbarian Gaul.

Bismarck saw, however, that something more than a large army, magnificently drilled, would be needed to maintain Prussian ascendancy in the German Empire. Although he regarded readiness for war as undebatable, he was too adept a statesman not to resent a little the assumption of the militarists that the State must be organized to serve the will of the Army, and that the Army must be called in to settle every international dispute. Bismarck knew that in his hands Diplomacy, without shedding a drop of blood, had won campaigns hardly less important to Prussia than those of Sadowa or Sedan. Why resort to a surgical operation at every moment, when the pharmacopœia of Diplomacy — bread pills, perhaps even hypnotism or a little poison — would serve?

The Teutonic lust for war having been developed to an unprecedented degree, Bismarck now set about evoking the spirit of vassalage — that other immemorial Teutonic heirloom. Responding to modern conditions, this took the form of a capacity for obedience and a submissiveness to discipline unexampled among any civilized race into whose ears the word Liberty had ever been whispered.

CHAPTER IV

MANIPULATING TEUTONIC TRAITS

Seest thou a man wise in his own conceit? There is more hope of a fool than of him. *Proverbs*, XXVI, 12.

A UNIVERSAL military service not only standardized German experience, by subjecting all German men during their impressionable years to the same sort of life and to a uniform drill, but it also deepened in them that atavistic craving for discipline, and that capacity for obedience, which made them both obsequious towards those above them and insolent towards those below. They lacked initiative: but they were patient, thorough, easily satisfied if they had sufficient sausage and beer for their stomachs and music for their ears. These Teutonic masses, which resemble in so many points the Chinese rather than any European race, were slowly organized into a machine as vast as Germany itself.

In industry, agriculture, and commerce discipline similar to that in the Army was established. Education came under the iron rule. The State subsidized the opera houses and theatres. There was no art, but there were many painters and sculptors who looked to official patrons for recognition. When the site of Berlin is again a wilderness for four-footed wolves and wild boars, the elephantine monstrosities which William II set up in the Siegesallee, to glorify his Hohenzollern forerunners, may remain to enlighten posterity as to the artistic sense of the Prussians when they decided to go forth and subjugate the world. The State Church had long been fossilized: in the Roman Church the Jesuits flourished.

Little by little the university professors, some through blandishments, some through rebukes and snubs, some by their own undisguised preference, became a wheel of the State machine. The professorial class, bred for the most part from the *bourgeoisie*, inherited the inborn German reverence for the titled classes, and its members were easily flattered by the bestowal of the Red Eagle or by the call to a chair at Berlin, and many a waverer seems to have been won over by a few condescending remarks from the Kaiser. Men formerly renowned for their independence now spoke the words they were expected to speak, and devoted their carefully trained intellects to discovering and proclaiming reasons for idolizing a régime which they had once abhorred. The deliberate perversion of the German universities by the Kaiser dealt a blow to the honor and scientific prestige of German professors from which they cannot soon recover. Posterity will judge them as it judges the Inquisitors who did the bidding of Philip II. On which the heavier blame, the corrupter, or those who eagerly allowed themselves to be corrupted?

Only one element in Germany, the Socialists, threatened for a brief time to accept no reconciliation with the Imperial Despotism. Their chief prophet, Marx, it should never be forgotten, had been obliged years earlier to seek shelter for his life and freedom for his utterances in England — England, hated by German Junkers and war-maniacs, not to mention Bismarck, the colossal Junker, and William II, the son of an English mother. Bismarck first tried persecution on the Socialists, and passed laws against them not less frightful than those which the Spanish Torquemada enforced against heretics; but when he saw the Socialists thrive under persecution, he adopted other tactics. He turned the flank of the Socialist movement by introducing a system which made Socialism dependent on the State. So the last organ which might possibly have served for whatever minority in Germany cherished Democratic or at least non-despotic ideals, was mitred into the despotic machine. Army and Navy, the Court, the far-reaching commercial and industrial interests, the banks, the press, the Church, the teachers and professors, the subsidized steamship lines, the railways, the Krupp factories, the Socialists, worked together as co-ordinate if not co-equal parts of the State.

In theory this State was an abstraction existing "above Society or the individual"— Germany, the Fatherland of all Germans, the ideal to which every German should consecrate himself; and the world will long marvel at the cunning by which the small Ring, which invented and worked this stupendous machine, caused the various parts of it to believe that they were each serving an ideal, when they were really serving that Ring. The real State was no abstraction: it was the Kaiser, the military clique, the Junker aristocracy, and their counterparts in other German provinces.

The German nation, obedient to the point of servility, seldom questioned what it was ordered to believe. If a few centrifugal persons ventured to criticize, they were quickly jailed. But the millions accepted their lot more than gladly, because they were convinced that the German Empire surpassed all others, and that the Germans — that is, themselves — were superior to any other race, past or present.

A spindle is but a spindle, though it work in the largest mill in the world; but the most insignificant German seemed to swell with the largeness of the entire German Empire. Self-conceit is an attribute of children and savages, in whom naïveté somewhat softens its repulsiveness. We are inclined to see only humor when a child or a Polynesian, out of his narrow experience, speaks boastfully. Men of genius, and especially men who imagined without sufficient warrant that they had genius, have also often been puffed up with self-esteem: but even among them the old fashion has changed, and they usually simulate modesty though they have it not. In a period like the Renaissance, when individualism ran riot and collapsed in hysteria, egotistic vanity flourished naked and unabashed.

One sign of a civilized nature, however, is self-knowledge; and self-knowledge teaches either an individual or a State that there are other individuals and other States, very different, it may be, but possessing qualities as excellent as those of their rivals. Difference does not necessarily imply inferiority; nor is self-reverence to be confounded with conceit. We should love our country and should be prepared to sacrifice our lives at the call of patriotism; but never should this love mislead us into thinking that ours is the only country, or the best. True patriotism is rather a passion like that which we feel for our family and friends, and no more depends on geographic or economic externals than the love of a child for its mother depends upon her beauty or her wealth.

Self-esteem has been so salient a characteristic of the Teutons, and especially of the Prussians, since the earliest times, that we may assume it to be innate in them. Perhaps it was sharpened when as Barbarians they swarmed into the civilization of the Roman Empire. They had no great cities, no marble temples, no Senate houses, no towering and luxurious baths; and so they pretended to scorn them, and to magnify their own barbaric dwellings and manners and customs. At any rate, their conceit survived every vicissitude.

The forays which the medieval German kings made recurrently into Italy did not, by introducing the Germans to peoples more civilized than themselves, suggest to them that their own ways and natures could be improved upon. Even the Reformation, which promised at the outset to give Germany not only leadership, but really close relations with the other Powers, soon became local, having in each country its peculiar form and special aims; so that the German States, disunited, discordant, dull, fell back into that parochial frame of mind in which egotism flourishes. It is a nice question whether egotism is more insufferable in those who are down or those who are up; the Prussians were equally arrogant, whether in victory or in defeat.

Frederick the Great sent to France for exemplars of civilized wit and manners; he spoke French, he wrote French; but his loyal subjects never took this as a hint that they were less civilized than the French, and Frederick himself did not object to their dulness and bad manners, so long as they furnished him the docile soldiers and bureaucrats whom he needed.

We can hardly lay too much stress on the German self-conceit as an important element in bringing Germany to the condition where she would embark exultingly in the Atrocious War. After 1870, a modest Prussian would have been an anachronism. The Empire stood at the head of Europe; its scholars led the world. It extended applied science, not only into the larger domain of industry, but into the concerns of daily life. It perfected, piece by piece, the immense machine, of which the Kaiser held the throttle. And when the word went forth from above that the Germans were the Chosen People, before whom a destiny of illimitable grandeur opened, hardly a German skeptic challenged that announcement, which merely confirmed what each of them and his ancestors had taken for granted, since Her-

mann vanquished the Romans in the Teuto-
burg forest. To keep playing on the chord of
egotism, which set every Teuton heart vibrating, was the obvious policy of the Imperial
Ring.

CHAPTER V

THE KAISER AND GOTT PARTNERSHIP

He created Gott in his own image.

BUT for the presence of William II, the ambition of the Imperial Ring might have waited long before it embarked recklessly on a world-war in order to gratify its ambition. We cannot yet say — perhaps posterity will never be able to determine — how far the Kaiser was unwittingly the tool of the Ring and how far he shaped it to his own purposes. At least we may be sure that the Ring would have thwarted him unless it had found him satisfactory. Had he attempted to establish a free government, for instance, his path would have been blocked by Junkers; or if he had acceded to the proposal of the other great Powers to restrict armament, he would not have been popular with the German military caste.

But there was never any likelihood that he

would do these or any other Liberal acts. He was a Hohenzollern through and through — one of the Hohenzollerns on whose stem the shoot of semi-savage Prussianism, grafted centuries before, had grown luxuriantly. His first object was to Prussianize Germany; his next, to Germanize the world. Versatile and neurotic, his conceit soon developed into unchecked egomania. At the outset, the minute German specialists smiled when he laid down the law to them in Biblical criticism, or in painting, in history, or in army tactics, or in a hundred other fields; but after a while they listened to him gravely, as to Sir Oracle. Their obsequiousness, which cost them little, brought them his favors for themselves and his backing for their enterprises. He Prussianized Germany in ways I have already hinted at, until the reluctant Bavarians or the suspicious Würtembergers came to regard Imperial German aggrandizement as the leading tenet in their patriotic creed.

William's egomania revolved on two wheels

— War and Statesmanship. The achievements of Napoleon as a soldier and of Bismarck as a statesman would not let him sleep. To the dire misfortune of Europe, he believed that he united in himself the genius of both those consummate men: and this he sought to demonstrate by his acts. He chose a succession of mediocrities as his Chancellors, with the result that the policies pursued were his policies. Bismarck had advised Germany to keep on friendly terms with Russia and with England; William antagonized both England and Russia without any apparent compensation, and accustomed the German people to the idea that England was an enemy that must be destroyed, and Russia a peril that must be removed. He used France as a pretext for augmenting the German Army, bullying her to the verge of desperation, and then saying in substance to the Germans: 'You see what wicked people the French are; how hate corrodes their hearts; how revenge is their ruling passion. I am a man of peace, but I shall not be able forever to restrain my noble Army from taking up the challenge of these insolent braggarts and making an end of them once for all.'

'My noble Army!' For a quarter of a century that was the Kaiser's invariable refrain. To fortify that Army he bent all his plans. He allowed military considerations to control his diplomacy. He made the military caste, whose truculence had long been a by-word, uppermost in the Empire; for like Frederick the Great he knew that the durability of the Hohenzollern dynasty rested on the Army. He need not fear Socialists and Democrats, Anarchists and plain Liberals, so long as he had an Army which at his bidding would shoot down a hundred or a hundred thousand of them. Having secured safety at home, he could turn to his plan for conquest abroad.

Diplomacy conducted by men infected by the itch of militarism cannot fail to be denatured. A manufacturing house which sent out a prize-fighter instead of a persuasive agent to solicit orders and to adjust claims among its clients would soon lack customers. As the Kaiser fostered the Prussian brand of Diplomacy, which begins by bullying and proceeds through insults to brutality, he could hardly have been surprised to discover, by 1910, that Germany had no disinterested friend in the world. Several governments were polite to her because they feared her; Austria was her submissive vassal, and Turkey gave her a bought amity, which might at any time be shifted to a higher bidder.

Listen to a few passages of the Gospel according to William II:—[1]

It is the soldier and the Army, not parliamentary majorities and votes, that have welded the German Empire together. My confidence rests upon the Army.

The most important heritage which my illustrious grandfather and father bequeathed to me,

[1] These quotations are taken from *The War-Lord*, compiled by J. M. Kennedy. (New York: Duffield & Co. 1914.) See also *The German Emperor as shown by his Public Utterances*. By C. Gauss. (New York: Scribners. 1914.)

and which I entered upon with joy and pride, is the Army.

Wherever the German Eagle has thrust his talons into a country, that country is German and will remain German.

The problems which proved insoluble to the Holy Roman Empire, the modern German Empire is in a position to solve. The means that enables it to do this is our Army.

Any opposition on the part of Prussian noblemen to their King is a monstrosity. Such opposition can be justified only when the King leads it.

Our German people will be the granite rock on which Almighty God will complete his building of the civilization of the world.

Only the German nation is left to defend and above all to cultivate great conceptions.

The soldier must not have a will of his own. He must have only one will, and that will mine.

A ruler may be very disagreeable, and I will be disagreeable if I think it necessary.

There is only one master in this country: I am he, and I will not tolerate another.

There is only one law — my law; the law which I myself lay down.

God will be on our side if ever our peaceful work is interrupted.

Hurrah for the dry powder and the sharp

sword, for the end we have in sight and the forces we are bending towards it, for the German Army and the General Staff!

Proud of the incomparable discipline and loyalty of its Army, Germany is resolved, without in any way threatening the rights of others, to maintain its Army at the degree of perfection it thinks necessary for the defense of its interests.

If we have been at peace for a long time, we owe our good fortune to our well-tried Army as well as to the favor of the Almighty.

The Army and the Emperor at its head can alone secure the safety of the Empire and the peace of the world.

Our future lies upon the water. Imperial power means sea power, and sea power and imperial power are dependent on each other.

The best word is a blow — the Army and Navy are the pillars of the State.

We are the salt of the earth; we must show ourselves worthy of our great destiny.

God liveth as of old. Our great Ally still reigneth, the Holy God, who cannot suffer sin and iniquity to triumph.

The King of Kings calleth for volunteers for the front.

If history should mention a German world-power, or a Hohenzollern omnipotency, we do not wish it to be said that it was obtained by the point of the sword, but by the mutual confidence of nations striving for the same ideal.

To multiply these utterances, dating from different years, would merely show the Kaiser's fertility in putting the same thoughts in various forms. The specimens quoted sum up his creed. He admonished his German subjects, and announced to the world, that he was the King of Kings; that he ruled by Divine Right; that he held in the hollow of his hand the life and death of every German; that the Army, with which he gradually associated the Navy, was the supreme institution in the Empire; that the Germans were the Chosen People, who might look forward to winning world-power and even omnipotence; that God was his Ally, who could be depended on in case of need to promote Imperial German ambition.

The substance of these doctrines was not original. Many despots, especially those who secretly dreamed of military expansion, have used similar phrases. The Jews were the Chosen People; and so have others declared themselves, with perhaps less justification. Autocrats have always assured their subjects —when, indeed, they condescended to give reasons of any kind — that they enjoyed a monopoly of Divine favor. Napoleon, more modest than the windy Prussian, talked about his "Star," thereby suggesting a sufficiently vague and imaginative idea and one less shocking than "God" to pious ears.

William's references to God reveal the bizarre medley of his moral nature. He did not need to go to Machiavelli to learn that a prince should use religion as an instrument for intensifying his subjects' obedience, or as a cloak to hide his own designs against other princes. William needed only to turn to the "Confessions" of Frederick the Great,[1] the Prussian

[1] *The Confessions of Frederick the Great* and *The Life of Frederick the Great by Heinrich von Treitschke.* Edited by D. Sladen; Foreword by G. H. Putnam. (New York: Putnams. 1915.)

Despot whom he most idolized, in order to find expressed with brutal frankness the diabolical creed which William himself has practiced.

Religion [says Frederick, in the Second Morning of his "Confessions"] is absolutely necessary in a state. . . . A king must know very little of politics, indeed, that should suffer his subjects to make a bad use of it; but then it would not be very wise in a king to have any religion himself. Mark well, my dear nephew, what I here say to you; there is nothing that tyrannizes more over the head and heart than religion; because it neither agrees with our passions, nor with those great political views which a monarch ought to have. The true religion of a prince is his interest and his glory. He ought, by his royal station, to be dispensed from having any other. He may indeed reserve outwardly a fair occasional appearance, for the sake of amusing those who are about him, or who watch his motions and character.

If he fears God, or, to speak as the priests and women do, if he fears Hell, like Louis XIV in his old age, he is apt to become timorous, childish, and fit for nothing but to be a Capuchin. If the point is to avail himself of a favorable moment for seizing a province, an army of devils, to defend it, present themselves to his imagination; we are, on that supposition, weak enough to think it an injustice, and we proportion, in our conscience, the punishment to the crime. Should it be necessary to make a treaty with other Powers, if we remember that we are Christians, we are undone; all would be over with us; we should be constantly bubbles. As to war, it is a trade, in which any the least scruple would spoil every-thing, and, indeed, what man of honor would ever make war, if he had not the right to make rules that should authorize plunder, fire, and carnage?

I do not, however, mean that one should make a proclamation of impiety and atheism; but it is right to adapt one's thoughts to the rank one occupies. All the popes who had common sense have held no principles of religion but what favored their aggrandizement. It would be the silliest thing imaginable, if a prince were to confine himself to such paltry trifles as were contrived only for the common people. Besides, the best way for a prince to keep fanaticism out of his country is for him to have the most cool indifference for religion.[1]

[1] The genuineness of Frederick's *Confessions*, or *Matinées*, as they were called in their first French edition, has been questioned. The passage quoted, however, accords with both his views and practices.

The man who thus instructed his nephew as to the use which a king should make of religion did not take the trouble to pay the tribute which civilized vice is supposed to pay to virtue: how could he, when he neither believed in virtue nor had the faintest conception of its meaning unless it coincided with a despot's plans? He was no more ashamed of his cynical treatment of the most sacred aspirations possible to man than savages are of their ceremonial orgies or their cannibalism. He was simply Prussian, enunciating the Prussian ideal, which, being Prussian, required no excuse.

Possessing neither Frederick's intellect nor his thorough-going contempt for mankind, William II was soft enough to like to appear good-natured on occasions when his autocracy was not in question; and even if he had not understood the value of Gott as a device for keeping the people under, he would probably have continued to harp upon Gott in order to gratify the popular instinct. When analyzed, the Prussian deity is seen to be in essence merely tribal, one of the deities of the Teutonic mythology — a combination of Odin and Loki — dressed in the uniform of Colonel of Pomeranian Grenadiers. This Gott, whom William had for a partner, seems in reality to have been William's double, who approved of the Kaiser's policies, invariably sided with him in war and peace, and, like William, lauded the Germans as the Chosen People. Though their reverence for the Kaiser would have sufficed to make them obey his commands, they were undoubtedly stimulated in their zeal when he told them that Gott thought just as he did. They could neither see nor hear the invisible partner, but the Kaiser's reports of him were too definite, not to say familiar, for them to be skeptical.

That William II's Gott should be a pagan of the old Germanic type was inevitable. Two generations of unparalleled devotion to scientific research and metaphysics had left Germany pagan and materialist. The stirring

of atavistic instincts in her, through the rediscovery by the historians of medieval Germany and their magnification of the glories of
medieval Hohenstaufen, Saxon, and Suabian
monarchs, turned German attention back still
further, to the time before Christianity had
replaced their pagan religion.

In a passage of singularly imaginative in-
sight, the late J. A. Cramb surveyed swiftly
the fourteen centuries during which the Germans called themselves Christians. There
was, he says, no real Christian spirit in their
hearts. Their religion was the religion of valor,
of war, of killing and being killed, of making
physical courage the final test of life, and its
attainment the only aim worthy of men. But
Christ preached a different religion — the
religion of righteousness, of brotherhood, of
self-sacrifice, and of mercy. The war to which
he called his followers was of the spirit, and
spiritual was the test which he applied to conduct; not to kill, but to heal; not to hate, but
to love; not to oppress, or cheat, or persecute

others, but to do unto them as you would be
done by — those were the ideals which Christ
opposed to the religion of Odin, the War-God.

Cramb puts into the mouth of latter-day
Germany this summary: —

Judæa and Galilee cast their dreary spell over
Greece and Rome, when Greece and Rome were
already sinking into decrepitude and the creative power in them was exhausted, when weariness and bitterness wakened with their greatest
spirits at day and sank to sleep again with them
at night. But Judæa and Galilee struck Germany in the splendor and heroism of her prime.
Germany and the whole Teutonic people in the
fifth century made the great error. They conquered Rome, but, dazzled by Rome's authority,
they adopted the religion and the culture of the
vanquished. Germany's own deep religious instinct, her native genius for religion, manifested
in her creative success, was arrested, stunted,
thwarted. But having once adopted the new
faith, she strove to live that faith, and for more
than thirty generations she has struggled and
wrestled to see with eyes that were not her eyes,
to worship a God that was not her God, to live
with a world-vision that was not her vision, and
to strive for a heaven that was not her heaven.

But struggle as she might, Germany found Christianity an alien religion. By the Reformation she freed herself from it in its most rigid theological discipline: and then she chafed at Protestantism. Her philosophers, from Kant to Nietzsche, pulled down one after another the pillars on which rested what remained of Christianity. Nietzsche freed Germany from the last trammels of Christian tradition.

Nietzsche clears away the "accumulated rubbish" of twelve hundred years [says Cramb, speaking for Germany]. He attempts to set the German imagination back where it was with Alaric and Theodoric, fortified by the experience of twelve centuries to confront the darkness unaided, unappalled, triumphant, great and free. . . . And what is the religion, which, on the whole, may be characterized as the religion of the most earnest and passionate minds of young Germany?

In the newer Imperative ring the accents of an earlier, greater prime, the accents heard by the Scamander, which even at Chæronea did not entirely die away:—

Ye have heard how in old times it was said, Blessed are the meek, for they shall inherit the earth; but I say unto you, Blessed are the valiant, for they shall make the earth their throne. And ye have heard men say, Blessed are the poor in spirit; but I say unto you, Blessed are the great in soul and the free in spirit, for they shall enter into Valhalla. And ye have heard men say, Blessed are the peacemakers; but I say unto you, Blessed are the war-makers, for they shall be called, if not the children of Jahve, the children of Odin, who is greater than Jahve.[1]

Such is the religion, described in flinty phrases by one who more than half believed in it, which Germany has been waiting for fifteen centuries to force upon the world at the point of her sword.[2] The deity who presides over this

[1] J. A. Cramb: *Germany and England* (London: John Murray, 1914), pp. 113, 114, 116, 117.

[2] The suspicion that the Germans would relapse to their primitive barbaric ideals, has haunted more than one of their writers. Heine expressed this in a memorable passage, from which these sentences are taken: "Christianity — and this is its most beautiful service — has subdued to some extent that German brutal desire for combat, and if the restraining Talisman, the Cross, falls to pieces, then the ferocity of the old fighters will break out, the senseless

religion is the Gott with whom William II is in partnership.

Berserker rage, about which the Northern poets say and sing so much. That Talisman is rotten, and the day will come when it will crumble away. Then the old stone gods will rise out of the desolate ruins and rub the dust of a thousand years from their eyes, and Thor will spring up with his giant hammer and dash to pieces the old Gothic cathedrals." Heine: *Sämmtliche Werke*, vol. III, p. 108, "Religion und Philosophie in Deutschland." (1834.)

CHAPTER VI

WILLIAM THE PEACEMAKER

A certain prince of the present time, whom it is well not to name, never does anything but preach peace and good faith, but he is really a great enemy to both.

MACHIAVELLI, *The Prince*, XVIII.

WILLIAM II became Emperor in 1888. He had nourished himself on the doctrines and example of Frederick the Great. The claim to reign by Divine Right, which the elder and the younger despot boasted, is a growth of comparatively recent centuries among European sovereigns, not without humor. Stripped of its bombastic rhetoric, it amounts simply to this: when a monarch had successfully established his power, by usurpation, by robbery, or by slaughter, he declared that he was God's anointed. William both liked the idea and knew its potency, even among a race which was fast losing its sense for the Divine in everything. The Romans, after the time of Augustus, sank into such moral decadence that they went further: they no longer traced the lineage of their Emperors to a divine ancestor, but treated them as gods in the flesh. William's inborn egomania was so pronounced that he might have found no difficulty in believing himself a deity; but while he always spoke in his own person as Emperor by Divine Right, he usually reinforced his commands by clinching references to Gott.

During the earlier years of his reign, his medievalism, his continual harangues on his own will and perfection, his louder and louder exaltation of the Army, his sudden outbursts of passion, or his diplomatic indiscretions, and the growing frequency with which he indulged in the disquieting amusement of rattling his scabbard, annoyed and even disgusted a good many Germans, especially those who lived outside of Prussia. One bold critic published a pamphlet on Caligula, in which he drew the portrait of the mad Roman Emperor so

vividly that myriads of Germans saw in it
the likeness of the divinely anointed, neurotic
Hohenzollern. The censors, however, soon
discouraged criticism by clapping into prison
satirists, editors, critics, and other doubters of
Imperial Almightiness. Even the most innocent could involuntarily commit the crime of
lèse-majesté: for the zealous Prussian officers
sniffed treason in trifles. The world laughed
irreverently to see the Germans laced in such
a strait-jacket and expected that they would
tire of William's despotic freaks; but he, and
also the Ring, which artfully poured into his
mind the suggestions of policies which he
supposed he originated, knew the Germans
best, and never doubted that they would
wear submissively the heaviest yoke, however restive they might be under a light
one.

Foreign observers, distrustful of William
from the beginning, were not less repelled by
his hypocritical praises of peace than by his
sanctimonious patronizing of Gott. Read over

his addresses and detect in them now, if you could not when he uttered them, their hollow note:—

The object of the Army is to secure peace for us, or if peace is broken, to be in a position to fight for it with honor.

I am determined to keep peace with every one, so far as it lies in my power.

The mighty German Army is the mainstay of the peace of Europe.

Though the German Navy is specially intended for the safeguarding and preservation of peace, it will, I am confident, do its duty if called into action.

Secure is that peace which stands behind the shield and under the sword of the German Michael.

I lend my hand to any cause which can help to further the great cause of peace.

I look upon the peace of the German people as sacred; but it is our duty to recognize from the signs of the times that we must prepare to defend ourselves from aggression.

The peace of Europe is not in danger: it rests on foundations which are too solid and firm to be easily shaken by the lies and calumnies of mischief-makers.

While the voluble William continued to vociferate "Peace, Peace!" he plotted "War, War!" in his heart. He went on unceasingly to swell his Army, to strengthen its equipment, and above all to encourage those who were diffusing the militarist poison in every German mind. As if it were not enough for Germans to be taught that they must be ready against the time when they should go forth to new victories on land, William breathed into them the dream that they ought also to dominate the sea. "Our future lies upon the water," he announced, at the opening of the new port of Stettin in 1890; words listened to with only a passing wonder, but which prove how early in his career the Kaiser was coquetting with the temptation of world-dominion. Thereupon the keels of the first German warships were laid down; the German Navy League was organized to arouse the enthusiasm of the Empire; the glory of embarking on vast colonial enterprises was preached; and the ulterior purpose which a mighty Navy might serve began to be whispered. By the year 1900 the toast, "The Day," was not only drunk by Army and Navy officers at their mess, but was proposed and cheered at public banquets.

What "Day"? The day on which the Germans should meet and destroy the English Navy, conquer England, shatter the British Empire, and inherit its wealth. That was the aim every German was taught to strive for; and, since we hate those whom we have injured or plot to injure, the German Mendacity Bureau circulated throughout Germany the belief that England, jealous of Germany's commercial success, intended to attack the Fatherland. So the business of teaching hatred of England was deliberately carried on, the black seeds being sown in the minds of little children and watered and nurtured with Teutonic persistence.

But actions speak louder than words, and during all those years when, under the pretense that England was going to attack Germany, Germany prepared to attack England, there was no port in the British Empire into which German merchant ships did not sail unhindered, no British dock on which German merchandise was not unloaded without discriminating duties. The Germans boasted, and with reason, of their industrial expansion, unmatched either in rapidity or in volume; they boasted that their goods undersold British goods in London itself; they boasted that they were taking away trade from England in China, in the Far East and in other British dependencies, as well as in other lands, to all of which they gained access through British ports. These boasts were founded on facts. And yet the Germans declared almost in the same breath that British "Navalism" — a word they coined to dupe the unthinking — prevented German industry from reaching a market and German commerce from having its share of the world's trade. In the long list of German lies few surpasses this in shamelessness. It would seem that to lie successfully one must be civilized. The German exercises in this art have the unconscious naïveté of the semi-savage, who fails to perceive either that he contradicts himself, or that his deceit is patent to his intended victim.

The favorite German practice of accusing the enemy of intending to do what the Germans themselves were on the point of doing, is another example of this semi-savage naïveté. In war they call it an "offensive defensive," and, since war is at best a relic of barbarism, the trick has its strategic justification; but in diplomacy or in politics its barbaric origin betrays it when it is tried on peoples whose standards are not semi-savage. The Kaiser and his Militarist Ring, however, used it with profit among the Germans themselves. When they wished to increase the Army, they needed only to whisper that Russia was threatening the Fatherland, or that France, stung by some German insult into uttering a fiery word, was growing dangerous and must be guarded against.

Having launched his naval policy, the Kaiser found England a convenient bogy for justifying the immense appropriations which his plans of naval expansion required. And while he added cruiser to cruiser and dreadnought to dreadnought, and reached at last the glory of the superdreadnought, he continued in his addresses to assure the world that the mission of the German Navy was peace. No doubt a great majority of the German people believed his assurances; no doubt, also, they believed that France and Russia and now England, either singly or together, were evolving the designs which the Imperial Ring insinuated against them. The German people have been trained too long to take their information from above, to question its veracity.

To Prussianize Germany; to keep the German military and naval equipment up to the highest pitch of excellence; to imbue the German people, whose obedience was proved past wavering, with such a sense of their supremacy that they would accept as a matter of course the gospel that they were to rule the world; and to proclaim himself the defender of peace, in order the more easily to mask his warlike projects — this was the work of William II, aided by his Militarist Ring, during more than twenty years of his reign. In these labors, patience stands out as the conspicuous trait. Hard must it have been for the innate autocrat, who, at twenty-five, imagined himself as being potentially a greater soldier than Napoleon — no less! — to wait one decade and then two, and well on into the third, for the opportunity to display his military genius. Many times he seemed to be on the point of breaking loose, but somebody always checked him at the last moment. Nevertheless, he allowed himself a certain luxury of pugnacious by-play, as if to hint to his Militarist entourage that he was not really a peace-loving milksop, and to warn foreigners that the scabbard he rattled held a sword, which he was aching to use.

In sending his telegram to the Boer Presi-

dent Kruger in 1896, he gratified his desire to
insult England. By seizing Kiao-Chau and assuming the protectorate over the province of
Shan-tung, he gave notice that Germany would
not lag behind the other European Powers in
land-grabbing. When the United States made
war on Spain, he did his utmost to form a
European coalition to protect Spain and to
punish the Yankees, whose Monroe Doctrine
thwarted his schemes in the Western Hemi-
sphere. He openly grieved that he had not a
large fleet, so that he might then and there
"take the United States by the scruff of the
neck." Deprived of that satisfaction, he sent
his preposterous Admiral Diederichs to Ma-
nila on the chance of clutching what he could
in the disintegration of the Philippines. Diederichs glowered upon the American Com-
modore Dewey in that enraged mastiff way
which seems to be taught to Prussian officers
as part of their drill; but Dewey was a simple
Vermonter, who had never been instructed
that he ought to quail at the Prussian glower,

and he quietly caused Diederichs to understand that, although his own ships were inferior in number and metal, he would attack the German squadron if it attempted to interfere. Diederichs understood.[1]

From that time forward, the Kaiser pursued a double policy towards the United States: in public, professing effusive friendship; in secret, chafing against the Monroe Doctrine which barred his projected German colonization in South America and checked his attempts by devious ways to secure a foothold from which the United States would find it hard to dislodge him. And then he abetted the scheme for organizing the German-Americans into a body which, at the favorable moment, should openly declare itself German and not American, defy the United States Government, and work to control this country in the Kaiser's interest. This conspiracy spread slowly, noiselessly, unobserved by its proposed victims, as

[1] It ought never to be forgotten that the British commander, Chichester, offered to stand by Dewey if there were need.

if it were a cancer which the Germans had the maleficent art to plant and nourish.

But while the Kaiser's hirelings sprinkled his poison secretly, he took delight in spectacular performances by which to startle the world. He sent a "punitive expedition" to China, and bade it treat the natives so frightfully that no Chinese would dare look a German in the face for a thousand years. Waldersee, who commanded the expedition, saw to it that the Imperial order "to be as Huns" was accurately carried out. Like the other European Powers, Germany expected to snatch a huge slice of China, but was deterred by the adroit diplomacy of John Hay, the American Secretary of State. The Kaiser's attack on Venezuela in 1902, intended nominally for the collection of debts due to Germans, but really to test whether the American Government would defend the Monroe Doctrine by something stronger than words, might have succeeded if a mere word-weaver had been President at Washington; but Theodore Roosevelt, also unterrified by the Prussian glower, insisted that the Kaiser must agree within forty-eight hours to submit the Venezuelan dispute to arbitration; and the Kaiser agreed.

It was in Europe, however, that William displayed his purposes most ominously. He detached Turkey from her long-standing bond with England. He extended Teutonic intrigues in the Balkans. Taking advantage of Russia's entanglement in the war with Japan, he bullied France and might have attacked her if he had not distrusted England's attitude. Still, he could plume himself on having humbled France and ousted her Foreign Minister, Delcassé, by merely rattling his scabbard. From that time on, although his truculence was less and less guarded, he did not desist from proclaiming that he held the maintenance of peace to be Germany's mission. In 1911 his patience seemed exhausted; for again he made French intrigues in Morocco a pretext for a bellicose demonstration, and he was on the point of invading France in order to achieve the long-threatened operation of "bleeding her white," when he discovered that England and Russia would support France and that his finances were less prepared than his Army. So again he drew back on the very brink of hostilities. Next year he demanded of every German a five per cent contribution — a "patriotic sacrifice" — for the benefit of the Army.

These specimen acts, told in sequence, and filled out, as they might be, by many symptomatic details, with the addition of other evidence not even referred to here, lay bare the speciousness of the Kaiser's claim to be reckoned among the peacemakers. He aspired to inherit the earth, but he was too good a Prussian to suppose he could come into that inheritance by peace instead of by war. And when put to the direct test of reducing the number of dreadnoughts to be built according to his naval program, or cutting down his Army, or entering into a conference on general disarmament, he flatly refused, and his mouthpieces in the press ridiculed these suggestions as childish.

CHAPTER VII

KULTUR

> When 't is God's will to bring an utter doom
> Upon a house, He first in mortal men
> Implants what works it out.
>
> ÆSCHYLUS. *Fragment* 151.

DURING Germany's long political and military preparation for world-supremacy, a propaganda for putting the minds and consciences of the German people into harmony with the Kaiser's ambition went on not less effectively, although it appeared to be less systematically organized.

Insatiate ambition, like jealousy, is a passion which gets confirmation and fresh fuel wherever it looks. In all directions the Germans saw proofs that they were the Chosen People. They interpreted the doctrine of evolution so as to draw from it a warrant for their aspirations. Evolution taught that "the fittest survived." Never was a word more decep-

tive than that word "fittest." When we apply
it to human concerns, which is fittest? Man
and the fly are widely diffused over the earth;
does that imply parity between them? A thug
can murder the wisest philosopher or noblest
statesman; the thug survives; does that mean
that he is "fitter" than his victim? The Germans believed that the first element in fitness
to survive is superior brute force. By that,
their ancestors had conquered decaying Rome;
by that, the Manchus made themselves masters of China; by that, the Spaniards over-
threw the more highly civilized Saracens. To
assemble the greatest possible volume of
brute force, in their Army, Navy, fortifica-
tions, and equipment, was therefore their
task.

A people which persuades itself that it is
not only superior but fittest, acquires inevitably a supercilious attitude towards the rest
of mankind; and during the last quarter of the
nineteenth century, when the Germans were
being infected by this idea, the other Great

Powers of Europe, and the United States also, accepted the doctrine that fate intended the Inferior Races to be the chattels of the Superior Races. To seize the lands of the black, brown, or yellow men who could not defend themselves, to exploit the natural resources of their lands, and to treat the black, brown, or yellow men as part of those resources, or even as a species of the fauna to be hunted and exterminated at will, was the cheerful, orthodox creed of the Superior Races. Material progress, which consisted in accumulating wealth at a speed hitherto unprecedented, was the standard which governed the Superior Races.

There is a venerable book which declares that God created man in his own image: this Book makes no mention of the color of God's creatures. But in our time white men have assumed that they alone are made in God's image and complexion, and that while they may be endowed with a soul, yellow and black and brown men are as soulless as the beasts of the field. The denial of human solidarity opens the door to hideous abuses.

The Germans laid to heart this fatalistic gospel of Superior and Inferior. With proper logic they argued that, since color was only an accident, the Superior Race had no more obligations towards an Inferior Race which happened to be white than towards a black or a yellow; and the evidences which satisfied them of their superiority, convinced them also of the inferiority of their white neighbors! By the German gauge, the Latins — Spanish, French, and Italians — were manifestly decadent. The Slavs, led by Russia, had never risen to civilization, but threatened to inundate Central and Western Europe. England, they had to admit, had been both a strong and a valiant nation; but she was weary now, with the weariness of old age, which deterred her from keeping up with modern methods, and she had become so enervated by wealth that she trusted in the gold of the sovereign, rather than in the steel of the sword. To

German eyes the United States appeared as a collection of eighty or ninety million human beings, the off-scourings of a score of countries, undisciplined, lacking a unifying principle, leaderless, corrupt, wayward, ominously good-natured, easily duped, and accessible to only one common motive — the desire of the dollar. To Germany, sure that she had the mission and the method, the task of subduing her white rivals, whose internal decadence she thought she had diagnosed, no longer appeared insuperable.

Ever since the Germans had taken to erudition, they had surpassed all their competitors as doctrinaires. Their passion for thoroughness, and their obedience to the word uttered from above, made them always seek for some theory to guide their thinking and their doing; indeed, they felt ill at ease until they had put on the stiff harness of some master theorist.

Their poets of the Golden Period sang somewhat vaguely of German unity and of free-

dom: not Goethe, who cared nothing for
either, setting humanity above patriotism;
but Schiller, whose soul was consumed by
his desire for liberty under the form of independence, and Arndt, and Körner, and other
patriotic voices. Then came the historians,
Giesebrecht, and Savigny, and the battalion
of other resuscitators of medieval Germany,
which they described with glowing detail and
with so much sympathy and admiration that
they caused their countrymen to turn for
example and for inspiration from the present
and look upon that past seen as in a rosy
mirage. It is a measure of the backwardness
of the Germans in political instinct, not less
than of that atavistic tendency of theirs to
which I have referred, that they could not
find a congenial resting-place in the politico-
social conditions of the nineteenth century,
but were at home only when they had re-
verted to the Feudalism of the eleventh. To
their satisfaction in the rediscovery of Medievalism presently was added the German

Imperial idea, another product of the glamorous Middle Age; then the spokesmen of Prussia, as the foreordained Imperial leader, arose; and finally, Prussia having created the German Empire, the subsidized historians, Von Sybel and the rest, sang their chorus of pæans to the House of Hohenzollern, and to the glories of Prussia, without which the German Empire — the dream of the medieval Teutons — could never have come to pass.

Art also conspired to glorify, not only German medievalism but Germanic mythology. Music, the only art which has flourished in Germany since Heine died, embodied through Wagner the medieval conceptions of Tannhäuser and Parsifal, and the semi-barbaric myths of the Nibelungen Epic — those myths in which fighting is the only honorable occupation for heroes on earth, and Valhalla the only heaven in which they hope to dwell. The mighty sweep of Wagner's compositions caused most of his hearers to forget that his themes reflected the unrestrained passions of

war, lust, and cunning that belong to an
uncivilized race. German erudites, to whom
everything German is superior to anything
foreign, assured their countrymen that "The
Ring of the Nibelungs" need not fear comparison with the "Iliad" and the "Odyssey";
but the millions who cared nothing for purely
literary discussions drank in the music like
wine, and through the intoxication it produced in them, they saw War and Valor, the
primitive ideals of their race, endued with
supernal magic. So Wagner's music hastened
the paganizing of the Germans, putting into
every German heart the pagan concepts out
of which he framed his Trilogy. At the same
time, although Wagner detested Prussia and
the Prussians, he helped on the Prussianiza-
tion of Germany, by reviving the atavistic
worship of Valor and War. Being wrought
subtly, these effects were all the more far-
reaching, penetrating even those musical
partisans who fought stubbornly against
Wagner's music. He might have paraphrased

the wise remark of Fletcher of Saltoun: "I care not who writes the laws of a nation, if I may write its operas."

In all this, the Germans were led, under the astute guidance of Prussia, back to those "old-German gloomy times" and ideals of "a barbaric past," which Goethe warned them against, instead of to the cheering and enlightening "eras in art and literature when remarkable men obtained perfect culture." No wonder that during the War the Prussian censors have put Goethe under the ban.

Still more was the Germanic megalomania stimulated by direct propaganda. Its high priests fished out of the waters of Lethe an "Essay on the Inequality of Human Races," written nearly forty years before by Count Arthur Gobineau, a French aristocrat, who thought that he had discovered the law which explains why some races dominate and others serve. "Understand the law, obey it and rule, and be saved by it from the decadence which has overtaken one dominant race after another" — that is the burden of Gobineau's message, which the Germans took to be addressed to themselves. What stronger backing could they desire than these deductions of the French prophet, who prophesied that the Gallic people would go down before the Teutonic? Gobineau Clubs sprang up, and Gobinismus poured its stream into the rising flood of Pan-Germanism.

But the Germans had a prophet of their own — Heinrich von Treitschke, nominally an historian, actually, the ablest partisan interpreter of history that Germany had seen. Like Carlyle, a volcano of ethical and political convictions, a fanatic, if you will, Treitschke, Slavic by descent, Saxon by birth, anti-Prussian by education, having been lured to Berlin, fell under the spell of the Prussianizing ambitions, and during the last twenty years of his life he taught thousands of receptive Germans from his professorial chair, and multitudes by his writings, that the German Empire could, and therefore must, move forward

to fulfil its transcendent destiny. By expos-
ing particularly the weakness of England,
he helped to implant hatred of her as an
irreconcilable rival to Germany. He assailed
also Democracy, and as he spoke with vigor,
which often became vituperative, he commanded attention; and as his message was not
less pleasing than Gobineau's to Teutonic
ears, his words supplied texts for Pan-Germanist promoters. His pupils became disciples, who carried his teaching to millions
who were entirely prepared to welcome it.
Treitschke, absolutely deaf, arrogant, insolent, stupendously self-centred and self-satis-
fied, closed his mental ears to adverse criticism; and well typifies the state of mind which
has prevailed in Germany under the fostering
methods of William II.

Philosophy also — if we admit that philosophy is *not* the love of wisdom — encouraged German megalomania. Nietzsche, another prophet of Slavic derivation, proclaimed
a creed which, if accepted literally, would

confirm the saying of the witty Frenchwoman that "the Earth is the madhouse of the universe." Indeed, long before Nietzsche was born, insane asylums in all countries swarmed with egomaniacs who had attempted to put Nietzschean principles in practice. Nietzsche held that the human race produces a few Supermen, the law of whose being is to make themselves stronger and stronger at the expense of the rest of mankind. Morals do not exist for the Superman, because morals are the disguised subterfuges of the weak to protect themselves from the strong. Finding themselves crushed by the might of the strong, the weak invented a system of good and evil, a moral code of right and wrong, according to which every one should be judged equally and the strong should be punished without fear or exception. The Superman must harden himself against the feeling of brotherhood, of compassion, of mercy, of charity. He must live "beyond good and evil"; he must accept no laws but the caprices of his own will, the

appetites and desires of his carnal nature, the
ambitions of what, were he a man, would be
called his soul. Nietzsche raged chiefly against
Christianity, which had constructed the religion under which slaves enjoyed rights and
Supermen were reminded of their bondage to
the moral law. The influence of Christianity
was further abominable because it enabled
the weak, the craven, the whimpering, to rise
to positions where they did not belong, and
kept alive masses who ought to be let die.
Since Supermen alone were to be considered,
whatever laid a featherweight of restraint
upon them was condemned.

In his own tragic pilgrimage to the mad-
house, Nietzsche flung out many other dog-
mas, often contradictory, but usually tainted
with egocentric extravagance. Like Wagner,
he loathed the Prussians, but that did not
prevent them from seizing upon his philosophy
of the Superman and applying it to themselves. Having once adopted it, they used
it as the keystone of their Pan-Germanist

designs.' Their racial self-conceit did not require to be persuaded that they were the Supermen outlined by Nietzsche; and whether the Kaiser ever read Nietzsche or not, he comported himself from the beginning of his reign as only one who recognized that he was a sublime Superman could.

A final argument came from the Militarists themselves. Early in the nineteenth century Clausewitz wrote the first scientific epistles on the worship of Moloch. His philosophy of War taught that War is necessary and normal, and that Peace, unless it be devoted to preparing for War, is a disease which cunningly saps the honor, strength, and even the life of a nation. No doubt the priests of Judah found reasons for persuading their countrymen to propitiate Moloch by the sacrifice of children, reasons which would seem crude to Germans filled with Hegelian intricacies, but not less abhorrent to the moral sense than are those of the latest Prussian rhapsodists of War. In this business, ancient

and modern lose their meaning, for War
makes all generations contemporary, and
Clausewitz's doctrines, which are dignified
by being called "philosophy," he might have
heard from Attila, and Attila might have
learned them from any wolf that possessed
the faculty of human speech.

It remained for General Friedrich von Bernhardi to describe baldly what Germany had
accomplished, what she stood for, and how
she could fulfil her mission. He wrote three
years before the Kaiser forced war upon the
world in 1914. Bernhardi was so brutally
frank that German apologists have tried to
disavow him, asserting that he was a person
of no consequence, an army officer in re-
tirement, who amused himself with his military vagaries, and they added that nobody
in Germany had read his book. Sheer false-
hoods. His book ran through many editions
before the war broke out; his own reputation as soldier and as military expert had long
been established; every one recognized that

he simply discussed matters which were the commonplaces of the General Staff and of the political Chancellery. And if he had never written, scores upon scores of other Germans had been pouring out for more than a decade articles, monographs, books, all fraught with the same message. Bernhardi wrote most clearly — that was the secret of his sudden and immense popularity.

His book, "Germany and the Next War," bears the stamp of authenticity in the utter unreserve with which it discusses projects which either shame or discretion might have counseled him not to divulge. In this respect it resembles Machiavelli's "Prince" and Frederick the Great's "Confessions." He takes it for granted that his readers are at one with him on his general proposition: that they will no more dispute the declaration that Germany must acquire world-dominion, and that she must resort to war to gain her ends, than a group of surgeons would wrangle over the necessity of surgery. Bernhardi's sole question was, when to perform the operation. Having demonstrated a nation's right to make war, he easily proves that it is a duty to make it, and then he so traces Germany's historical development as to arrive at the conclusion that the time is at hand for her to risk everything in a gigantic struggle. World-dominion or downfall — these are the alternatives which Germany must face. He has nothing but contempt for a nation which, having come within striking distance of world-dominion, hesitates or turns back.

The last part of his book is practical, in contrast to the doctrinal quality of the first part. He takes up questions of armament, of the navy, of the forces Germany can muster and those of her enemies, of political conditions at home, of diplomatic relations abroad, of finance, and of so manipulating the German people that they will regard the war, when it comes, as inevitable, and as being forced upon them by jealous and wicked rivals, and that they will support it with patriotic zeal. He

points to England as the chief adversary, but,
as if to dispel any unjustifiable respect Germans might still feel for England as a Great
Power, he describes her military feebleness,
her internal unsoundness, the senile palsy
creeping through her body and shaking her
will. Only in her navy is she still preëminent;
but he thinks that Germany can equal her in
naval material and in training and surpass
her in cannon, and by torpedo boats work
great damage to her fleet.

Bernhardi's discussion of the best plan of
campaign is not less lucid than his examination of the various alliances which might be
formed and how to deal with each. But the
significance of his book lies in the fact that
it is the revelation of the purpose of the German Imperial Despotism to rule the world,
and of the preparations made therefor. We
might call it "German Militarism in the Confessional," except that confession suggests the
recognition of having sinned, whereas the
German Militarists, from the Kaiser down,

instead of compunction, felt only such impatience as train-robbers may feel who, having perfected every plan, count the moments for the train to heave in sight.

Bernhardi quotes many laudations of war,[1] beginning with Heraclitus of Ephesus, who said, "War is the father of all things."

Here are other mottoes:—

War is as necessary as the struggle of the elements in nature. (A. W. von Schlegel.)

Wars are terrible, but necessary, for they save the State from social petrifaction and stagnation. It is well that the transitoriness of the goods of this world is not only preached but is learned by experience. War alone teaches this lesson. (Kuno Fischer.)

A thousand touching traits testify to the sacred power of the love which a righteous war awakes in noble nations. (Treitschke.)

War opens the most fruitful field to all virtues, for at every moment constancy, pity, magnanimity, heroism, and mercy shine forth in it. (Frederick the Great.)

[1] I quote from the English Popular Edition. F. von Bernhardi: *Germany and the Next War*. London: Arnold. 1914.

It has always been the weary, spiritless, and exhausted ages which have played with the dreams of perpetual peace. (Treitschke.)

As an unanswerable argument for any one who may still be bound by the tradition that Christianity enjoins love and peace, Bernhardi, with a deviltry at which Mephistopheles would chuckle, adds:—

Christ himself said: "I am not come to send peace on earth but a sword." ... Thus, according to Christianity, we cannot disapprove of war in itself, but must admit it is justified morally and historically.

I add a few of Bernhardi's own dicta, chosen almost at random: they express not only his individual opinions, but those of the Ring which has shaped the policy of modern Germany.

Since almost every part of the globe is inhabited, new territory must, as a rule, be obtained at the cost of its possessors — that is to say, by conquest, which thus becomes a law of necessity. ... Over-populated countries pour a stream of emigrants into other States and territories. These submit to the legislature of the new country, but try to obtain favorable conditions of existence for themselves at the cost of the original inhabitants with whom they compete. This amounts to conquest.

The conception of the constitutional State in the strictest sense is an impossibility, and would lead to an intolerable state of things.

There never have been, and never will be, universal rights of men.

· Even if a comprehensive international code were drawn up, no self-respecting nation would sacrifice its sense of right to it.

Arbitration treaties must be peculiarly detrimental to an aspiring people which has not yet reached its political and national zenith, and is bent on expanding its power in order to play its part honorably in the civilized world.

We are facing a hidden, but none the less formidable crisis — perhaps the most momentous crisis in the history of the German nation. We have fought in the last great wars for our national union, and our position among the Powers of *Europe;* we must now decide whether we wish to develop into and maintain a *World-Empire,* and procure for German spirit and German ideas that fit recognition which has been hitherto withheld from them.

In one way or another, *we must square our account with France*, if we wish for a free hand in our international policy. This is the first and foremost condition of a sound German policy, and since the hostility of France once for all cannot be removed by peaceful overtures, the matter must be settled by force of arms. France must be so completely crushed that she can never again come across our path.

No people is so little qualified as the German to direct its own destinies, whether in a parliamentarian or republican constitution; to no people is the customary Liberal pattern so inappropriate as to us.

Our own country, by employing its military powers, has attained a degree of *Kultur* which it never could have by the methods of peaceful development.

War is only a means of attaining ends and of supporting moral strength.

The first and most essential duty of every great civilized people is to prepare for war on a scale commensurate with its political need.

When public opinion does not stand under control of a master will, or a compelling necessity, it can be too easily led astray by the most varied influences. This danger is particularly great in a country so torn asunder, both internally and externally, as Germany.

Our western frontier, in itself strong, can be easily turned on the north through Belgium and Holland. No natural obstacle, no strong fortress, is there to oppose a hostile invasion, and neutrality is only a paper bulwark.

We shall therefore some day, perhaps, be faced with the necessity of standing isolated in a great war of the nations . . . and shall have to trust to our own strength and our own resolution for victory. Such a war — for us more than for any other nation — must be a war for our political and national existence. This must be so, for our opponents can only attain their political aims by almost annihilating us by land and by sea. If the victory is only half won, they would have to expect continuous renewals of the contest, which would be contrary to their interests. They know that well enough, and therefore avoid the contest, since we shall certainly defend ourselves with the utmost bitterness and obstinacy. If, notwithstanding, circumstances make the war inevitable, then the intention of our enemies to crush us to the ground, and our own resolve to maintain our position victoriously, will make it a war of desperation. A war fought and lost under such

circumstances would destroy our laboriously
gained political importance, would jeopardize
the whole future of our nation, would throw
us back for centuries, would shake the influence
of German thought in the civilized world, and
thus check the general progress of mankind in
its healthy development, for which a flourishing
Germany is the essential condition. Our next
war will be fought for the highest interests of
our country and .of mankind. This will in-
vest it with importance in the world's history.
"World power or downfall!" will be our rally-
ing cry.

We Germans have a far greater and more ur-
gent duty towards civilization to perform than
the Great Asiatic Power [Japan]. We, like the
Japanese, can only fulfil it by the sword.

There can only be a short respite before we
once more face the question whether we will
draw the sword for our position in the world or
renounce such position once and for all. We
must not in any case wait until our opponents
have completed their arming and decide that
the hour of attack has come.

Bernhardi wrote this last warning in October, 1913, and in July, 1914, the Kaiser and
his Ring decided that Germany's opponents

were in such unfavorable conditions that her
hour of destiny had struck. Then ensued the
Atrocious War, which had been prepared for
with more persistence, more thoroughness,
more ingenuity, and over a longer time, than
any other in modern history.

This war sprang as naturally from the German heart and will as a vulture springs from
its nest. Prussian egomania, which had succeeded in identifying German national interests with its own; the example of Frederick
and Moltke and Bismarck; the impassioned
gospel of Treitschke; the comforting reminder
of Nietzsche that to be a Superman, you
must act like a Superman; the demonstration
of Bernhardi that Germany must not longer
postpone her battle for World-Dominion;
and the Hohenzollern dynastic ambition, cir-
culating through every artery and vein of the
Empire — were elements, symptoms, omens,
that can neither be denied nor explained away.
Of course, we must remember that Kant,
Fichte, and Hegel — especially Hegel, with

his ideal of the State — had preceded; but it is the men who translate theory into action whom we hold responsible. The mind of the disciple, like an imperfect lens, distorts the teaching of the master.

CHAPTER VIII

PRUSSIANIZING GERMANY

Look to the essence of a thing, whether it be a point of
doctrine, of practice, or of interpretation.

MARCUS AURELIUS, VIII, 22.

CIVILIZED peoples have invariably cherished an ideal, which they call Culture
— it might be of the intellect; it might be
of the soul.

The culture which affects the soul is two-
fold, according as it lays greater stress on
Goodness or on Beauty. "To make reason
and the will of God prevail," as Bishop Wilson expressed it, is the end of ethical culture;
and life thus conceived becomes, in Arnold's
phrase, a "study of perfection." The definition of Culture which springs from Beauty,
or has Beauty for its special quest and desire,
evades a formula. Like Marlowe, we still ask:
"What is beauty?" But we recognize Taste
as the product of this culture. In actual life,

however, we seldom disturb ourselves over these nice distinctions. We see men who are cultivated chiefly on the side of intellect; others we think of in terms of goodness, lovers of their fellow men, seekers after moral and social perfection; and we know those whom metre or music or color or form sets vibrating — the artists.

The ideal man possesses taste and sympathy, the qualities common to all of these. He is not a specialist — for to be a specialist almost inevitably limits open-mindedness and sympathy. He is cultivated rather than learned; and nothing about him, not even his talk, will appear salient or aggressive, but all will be natural, and whatever he has acquired from learning, life, or art will flow from him as simply as fragrance from a flower. By his manners you shall know him — manners which register self-control and kindliness, justice, magnanimity, and fairness.

That is not Culture which does not eventuate in the gentleman. A glow of chivalry clings about it. We see it in Sir Philip Sidney's beautiful, simple courtesy to the dying soldier. It can manifest itself through the highest heroism and through the contacts of everyday life. Although known by what it avoids doing, it is as affirmative as sunshine or as health. But why multiply phrases when Culture speaks for itself?

Culture of the broad and hospitable kind has found only a scanty soil in Germany, and until Goethe came, it had in fact hardly sprouted there. In a community where the standards of living not less than of learning lagged behind those of Germany's neighbors, Goethe's insatiate curiosity soon exhausted its German provender and seized upon the Renaissance and Classical Antiquity to enrich his poetic genius. But the culture which Goethe exemplified better than any other modern was that of an Olympian egotism. Cultivate yourself for yourself; act as if the law of *your* being were universal law: does not this advice underlie the Goethean system?

Goethe quickened wide interests among the Germans, and contributed more than all of them combined to the store of world-literature; but the culture which they learned from him was the culture of erudition and of egotism. They ransacked the libraries for subjects great and small, inspected each through the microscope, held post-mortems on every figure in art, letters, science, and history, and buried each under a mound — in Goethe's case, a mountain — of treatises, through which we tunnel with difficulty, if at all, to the original. The German passion for thoroughness stood between them and Culture of the higher sort, that Culture with which the qualities of a gentleman, not those of a pedant or a soldier, are inherently associated. It is significant that the German language has no word for gentleman. The gentleman cannot be created by pinning an iron cross or a red eagle on the lapel of an army officer or of a university luminary, or by dubbing him "von."

With the expansion of science, in which the Germans took a leading part, the idea of Culture as a possession of the soul dwindled away, and in its place loomed up Kultur, a product of the intellect. For a while Kultur meant to the Germans Civilization, "that complex whole which includes knowledge, belief, art, morals, law, custom, and any other capabilities and habits acquired by man as a member of society." But little by little Kultur, when used in reference to matters German, acquired a restricted meaning. It no longer concerned the individual, nor did it suggest personal refinement. Kultur meant specifically the system which ruled Germany, and as that system became Prussianized, Kultur was Prussianized. During the past twenty years its definition has been: Whatever strengthens the German Empire under the dynasty of Hohenzollern is Kultur.

The Army, therefore, as William II has reiterated throughout his reign, is the cardinal instrument and prop of Kultur, and the

Krupp howitzer is its fittest emblem. Education, which taught submissiveness and instilled into the youngest pupil the commandments of Kultur, came next, but an unbridgeable abyss separated the educators from the privileged militarist class. To the German people, as we have already witnessed, such discrimination seemed proper, and to the Prussians the idea that the monarch should be despotic was as natural as that a tiger should be striped. Frederick the Great on his walks through Berlin used to cane any burgher whose aspect happened to displease him; and his loyal Berliners, instead of being incensed, may have felt honored by the chastisement. William II used more insidious means than caning to express his displeasure; but the disposition on the part of the Prussians to accept whatever the monarch deigned to bestow, was not less subservient than in Frederick's time.

The guiding principle of Kultur is unquestioning duty to the State. Its aim is Efficiency, and never has another nation brought Efficiency to such perfection. But to what purpose? Culture, according to Arnold, strives "to make Reason and the will of God prevail." Kultur, on the contrary, aims to make the German Empire under the House of Hohenzollern prevail; it would be rash to identify either of these with Reason and the will of God.

From whatever angle we have looked at the Germanic development in recent generations, our vision has always fixed, sooner or later, on an impenetrable core of egotism which easily swells to arrogance, and from arrogance to insolence. The victories of 1870 gave cause for military exultation. German scholarship had the cry, and no German professor would admit that he could think of himself more highly than he ought to think. The German imagination peopled the past with vague and vast achievements performed by heroes — German, always German — more than mortal.

Coming very late into the comity of nations, the Germans were at the disadvantage of nourishing their minds on their home-made philosophy and literature of yesterday or today. Now, if their philosophers had been Plato and Aristotle, and their poets Dante and Shakespeare, the fact that they were almost if not quite contemporary would have detracted somewhat from their value as guides. The Germans bred in and in, a process which leads to egomania if not to insanity. The Englishman is insular, but his traditional training in the Classics and his transactions in the world's business have given him that breadth of view which comes from knowing intimately the history and ideals of great races far removed in time and blood from ourselves, and from actual cosmopolitanism. So was it with the Puritans, who fed on the Bible, which, besides providing them with their religion, unfolded to them also the ways of remote but mighty races.

The recent German, on the contrary, has

been brought up to suppose that whatever was not German was inferior, to be tolerated only until it could be replaced by a German product, or, if not replaced, destroyed. Not content with puffing themselves up, the Germans have lately listened complacently to zealots who claim that it was a hidden Germanicism in Dante, Shakespeare, and other foreign masters [1] which made them great, and that even Jesus Christ was honored by having a strain of Teutonic blood in his veins. If certain grave professors tell the truth, there have been only two literatures worthy of consideration — the German and the Greek.

[1] See Ludwig Woltmann's treatises. Vinci, he asserts, is plainly the German Wincke; Vecellio is Vetzel; Buonarotti is Bohnrodt! He claims as Germans many French celebrities — Lafayette, Pascal, Voltaire, Cuvier, Descartes, Robespierre, Balzac, Musset, Lamartine, Hugo, Zola, and many others. Even if these claims were established, should we not ask: Why has Germany produced no Titians and Michael Angelos and Leonardos herself? Why no Voltaires and Balzacs and Hugos? If these types of genius appear in Italy and in France and not in Germany, a non-Kultured logic would deduce that it must be the Italian or the French strain in the blood, and not the German, which produced them.

To paraphrase what Whistler said of Nature, "Why drag in the Greek?"

A man who spends his life looking at himself in the glass cannot fail to reach the conclusion that he is unique, perfect, the pattern and standard of all men. This has been Germany's attitude for five-and-twenty years. Although Germans have traveled to all parts of the earth, establishing industrial colonies, prospecting for commercial enterprises, or filling professors' chairs, they have been so swallowed up by their Germanism that they have not understood the natures of the peoples among whom they moved. To a German the "psychology" of every one else is a sealed book. How could it be otherwise? For between the German and you and me, when he looks at us, there is the mirror, invisible to you and me, in which he is doting over his own features.

Far, indeed, has Kultur strayed from Culture — Kultur so repulsively self-bloated, wearing its ego on the outside, as the turtle wears its skeleton, till it becomes thick, indurated, and at last, impenetrable; Culture, which looks beyond itself, seeks the best wherever it exists, recognizes the validity of different standards, and practices tolerance without in the least surrendering convictions. As Kultur has trumpeted its own praises everywhere, it is unnecessary to cite many specimens of it. I content myself with quoting a few lines from a letter written to a friend in Holland by Dr. Adolf Lassen, Professor of the Love of Wisdom (Philosophy), at the University of Berlin. The letter was written in the third month of the war: —

No one can remain neutral to the German State and people. Either you must consider it the most perfect creation that history has produced up to now, or you acquiesce in its destruction; nay, in its extermination. A man who is not a German, knows nothing of Germany. We are morally and intellectually superior beyond all comparison as to our organizations and our institutions. . . . Our Army is the epitome of German excellence.

As Professor Lassen was eighty-four years old when he wrote this, we have a right to assume that his opinions were deliberate and mature, free alike from the exaggerations of a callow partisan and from the explosive fury of a young fanatic.

When an octogenarian, delivering himself in this fashion, represents the whirling thoughts of an entire nation, war must be imminent. The only alternative to war would be the insane asylum: but even Germany, with all her preparation, had made no provision for locking herself up. If a man tells you that he is the most perfect creation on earth, the sacred vessel in whom is preserved the essentials of the highest civilization, you dissemble your amusement and pass on. For a nation to make such a boast without blushing — Kultur never blushes — portends evil.

The stages by which Kultur led up to war are thus plain. First, it Prussianized the German people, by teaching the non-German

States that the interests of the Empire coincided with those of Prussia. Next, it kept assuring the Germans that they were the most marvelous of all races, an assertion which they had no reluctance in believing. And then Kultur preached that the other Powers, secretly conscious of their inferiority, were devoured by jealousy of Germany's superiority, and that, foreseeing that they must go down before it, they formed a league to ward off their own destruction by crushing Germany. This suggestion, artfully insinuated and repeated every day from all quarters throughout many years, became an overwhelming obsession.

The German Army, with the Krupp howitzer as its highest product, embodied Kultur; and the nation, obsessed to the point of fury, felt relief from suspense when its masters hurled the Army against the league of foes.

CHAPTER IX

HOW THE ATROCIOUS WAR BEGAN

Forgetful is green earth; the Gods alone
Remember everlastingly: they strike
Remorselessly, and ever like for like.
By their great memories the Gods are known.
  GEORGE MEREDITH: *France: December, 1870.*

THE Kaiser and his Ring have not been able to evade the guilt of beginning this war. The inky stream, which, like the cuttle-fish, they have emitted in their efforts to escape, has not availed them. Their garbled or faked documents, slyly mixed in with bits of genuine evidence, have been exposed. After all, however, in fixing the responsibility for a vast conflict, the historian seeks to know, not only who kindled the spark that set off the explosion, but also who accumulated the powder to be exploded, and who would benefit most by the explosion.

On their own confession, the Germans have been for years fully prepared for war. "Hur-

rah for the dry powder and the sharp sword,"
the Kaiser shouted long ago; "for the end we
have in sight and the forces we are bending
towards it, for the German Army and the
General Staff!" And on another occasion he
declared: "The Teuton never fights better
than when he is called upon to defend himself
on all sides. So let our enemies begin. We
are ready for them all!"

Nobody has questioned Germany's material preparedness. But what of her will, what
of her desires? Has she been harboring reso-
lutions of peace? Has she been contented with
her position as one of the European Powers?
Has she never hinted that her increase in
population not less than her industrial expansion called for territorial and colonial aggrandizement? Who was it that declared, as far
back as June 18, 1891: "In spite of the fact
that we have no such fleet as we should have,
we have conquered for ourselves a place in the
sun. It will now be my task to see to it that
this place in the sun shall remain our undis-

puted possession . . . for our future lies upon the water"?

The desire and the will to conquer were in the hearts of the Germans. The other Powers — England, France, and Russia — would unquestionably have been glad to see Germany humbled; but neither singly nor in coalition would they attack her; and, with what seems now fatuous trustfulness, the English, at least, refused to believe that the Germans would carry out the project towards which their preparation pointed. Since 1905, the agreement entered into by the Triple Entente — England, France, and Russia — aimed at mutual defense in case Germany should assail any of them. The will to attack dwelt in the Kaiser and his military chiefs. Their sole concern was to choose the propitious moment.

Why did they regard the last of July, 1914, as the appointed time? William's golden opportunity came in 1905 when Russia, in a death-grapple with Japan, could not assist

France, which he wished then to shatter beyond recovery. But he did not feel quite sure of England's neutrality; and as France bowed her head at his threats, he decided to sheathe his sword, and during the next seven or eight years he contented himself with rattling his scabbard.

The Balkan War of 1912 bristled with international asperities, any one of which might have served as an excuse to the great Powers for entering the conflict; but they refrained. The next year, however, Germany thought the time ripe. Austria, her willing vassal, acquiesced, and sounded Italy, their partner in the Triple Alliance; but Italy refused to join them, because they were bent on a war of conquest, whereas the terms of partnership required Italy's coöperation only for a war of defense.

When 1914 came, William II determined to wait no longer. He planned that Austria should be his cat's-paw to reduce Servia to vassalage, and so both to push forward Teu-

tonic ascendency in the Balkans and to humil-
iate Russia, as Austria, abetted by Germany,
had humiliated her in 1909 by annexing Bos-
nia and Herzegovina. The conditions as he
and his Ring saw them were so favorable that
it mattered little what Italy did. Of his own
strength he had no doubts. The German
Army had been increased, and the fruits of
the five per cent patriotic contribution had
served in many ways to complete preparations. The Kiel Canal, which as a means of
naval strategy was worth more than several
dreadnoughts, had been dedicated in June
and was in perfect running order. The German Navy itself, although evidently inferior
to the British, seemed to the eager Kaiser so
formidable that it might play a great part in
the war.

But the unreadiness of his enemies, rather
than his own strength, persuaded him. France
was reducing her term of military service,
and with it, in the opinion of many critics,
the efficiency of her Army. It was no secret

that she had reached the limit in her conscription. Her lack of artillery and other equipment was so notorious that Deputy Humbert had publicly exposed it in the Chamber of Deputies. An unsavory scandal, involving even Cabinet Ministers, aroused fierce dissensions and was construed as a symptom of a far-reaching corruption which would paralyze national energy, if a sudden call were made upon it. In Russia, also, internal unrest seethed. Several hundred thousand strikers at St. Petersburg had to be quelled by the troops. German spies had doubtless reported that Russia's store of munitions would not suffice for a long campaign. Worse still, Russia was just midway in changing from the old to the new army system. The Russian strategic railways, planned to enable her to pour her millions of soldiers on to the German and Austrian frontiers, would not be finished till 1917 — a fact which warned William to make haste.

Although he appears to have felt a slight

uncertainty as to England's probable course, he believed that the odds lay greatly against her breaking away from her traditional neutral policy. Early in May, he instructed his Ambassador at London, to discover if he could — without allowing his purpose to be suspected — whether, in case of a general Continental war, England would fight or not. Prince Lichnowsky, his Ambassador, is said to have sent a most reassuring report, in which he showed that Great Britain was in no condition to fight. Her quarrels over Home Rule and Ulster had reached the verge of civil war; party strife had fomented discord so bitter that no united national action was to be looked for; labor was in revolt; the pusillanimity of the Cabinet could be measured by the extent to which a handful of Suffragettes had terrorized it and the country. Underlying all was the fact, amply proved by the Boer War, that the English had ceased to be a martial people. Wealth, sapping their valor, made them prefer peace, the condition which promotes wealth.

So the Kaiser could push Austria into war with a light heart. Needing a pretext, he pitched upon the assassination of the Austrian Crown Prince by a Serb, and encouraged Austria to make demands so exorbitant that, if Serbia assented to them, she would virtually forfeit her independence. Throughout the month of July such warlike preparations went forward in Germany as would not excite suspicion. Forebodings, doubts, rumors, came and went in the European press, but they seemed baseless, and the public refused to believe that the murder of a single individual, even though he were an Austrian Archduke, would lead to war. Pretending that the matter concerned Austria alone, Germany kept herself aloof, only insisting that Austria should have a free hand. In spite of these German denials of collusion, there is ample reason to believe that the Kaiser, about the middle of July, saw and approved Austria's ultimatum to Serbia, and then he went off yachting in order to create the impression that he was not implicated in the negotiations which were designed to make war inevitable. These subterfuges had so quieting an effect outside of Germany and Austria, that European diplomats and foreign ministers began to think of summer vacations. The French President, indeed, cruised in the Baltic and paid an official visit to the Czar.

On July 23 the Austrian ultimatum was delivered at Belgrade. The next day Europe took a sudden anxious interest in the affair. At six o'clock in the evening of July 25 the Austrian Minister at Belgrade, having barely glanced at it, stated that, since Serbia's response to the ultimatum was not satisfactory, he was instructed to break off diplomatic relations. That same night, while he and his staff were traveling to Vienna, Austria issued orders to mobilize the army. And yet Serbia had conceded nearly all the demands of the Austrian Empire, except that which meant the extinction of her national independence. The brave little kingdom, recently wasted by two terrible wars, numbered only five million inhabitants; Austria had more than fifty million.

From the moment the ultimatum was sent, France and England urged Austria to consider the possible fearful results of carrying out her threat. They also urged Germany to bring pressure to bear on her Austrian vassal. Russia made it clear enough that she did not desire war, but that she would not allow Serbia to be crushed. Austria took a high-handed attitude.

Suddenly, on the evening of July 26, Emperor William returned to Berlin. As he entered the room where the military and cabinet chiefs were conferring, the Crown Prince said to him, sarcastically: "Father, you arrive too late!" It having been tacitly agreed that they should make war inevitable during the Kaiser's absence, — to shield him, — they did not wish him to muddle what they had done.

But the Over-War-Lord could be trusted to seize the occasion which he had impatiently waited for during many years. He sent evasive telegrams to his cousins, King George of England and Czar Nicholas of Russia. So far as appears, neither he nor Chancellor Bethmann-Hollweg nor Foreign Secretary Jagow had hinted to Austria, not that she should soften her demands, but even that she should refrain from pressing them for a few days. The Kaiser insisted that it was none of Europe's business whether Austria trounced Serbia or not; and so he logically approved of Austria's mobilization, while declaring to the Czar that if Russia mobilized, mediation would be "threatened if not made impossible." The Czar gave his solemn promise that as long as negotiations between Austria and Serbia continued, his troops would undertake no provocative action.

Suddenly, for some reason still unexplained, on July 31, Austria consented to enter into informal "conversations" with Russia — an indication, optimists thought, that war might be averted; because up to the day before she had insisted that her dealings with Serbia were a private affair, which she would discuss with nobody else. Who at Vienna suddenly waked up to the fact that the War Cabal in the Army and Cabinet, in collusion with the German Ambassador, was involving Austria, not merely in a brush with the Serbian pygmy, but in a European War of incalculable scope? Even a day's delay for "conversations" might check the militarist plunge into war.

William, however, although he knew of Austria's offer to "converse," frustrated this eleventh-hour hesitation, and saw to it that war should come. At midnight on July 31 he telegraphed an ultimatum to St. Petersburg, saying that, unless Russia ceased within twelve hours all warlike measures against both Germany and Austria, Germany would mobilize. Only one construction can be placed on this ultimatum — William purposed that it should force Russia to fight. When Russia allowed the twelve hours to elapse without obeying William's command, he declared war upon her. On that same July 31 the German Ambassador in Paris addressed a menacing communication to the French Government, demanding to know within eighteen hours whether France would remain neutral in case of war between Germany and Russia. Declining to give any pledge, Viviani, the French Prime Minister, simply stated that France would consult her own interests.

On August 2, the German troops went swarming through Luxemburg, and massed on the Belgian frontier. Germany postponed formally declaring war, although she was actually at war, in the hope that some chance shot might justify her in asserting that France began hostilities.[1] The Kaiser resorted to this guile, which was as transparent as it was specious, in order to hold Italy to those terms

[1] German apologists subsequently laid great stress on the report that two French officers were seen motoring on a Belgian road before war was declared!

of the Triple Alliance which bound her to
join the Teutonic Powers in case they were
attacked. The Italians were not deceived.
By their refusal to be drawn into the war of
aggression, the Teutons stand convicted.

This long record of Germany's preparation
for the war leaves no doubt as to her guilt.
If any persons are still duped into thinking
the Kaiser sincere when he protested his love
of peace, let them explain why he did not, as
a friend, dissuade Austria from flinging at
Serbia the firebrand ultimatum. Let them
explain why, when the firebrand had been
hurled and Austria was bombarding Belgrade,
he declared truculently that the affair did not
concern Europe, and intimated that he would
allow no meddling. When had Europe au-
thorized him to prescribe for her the limits
of her jurisdiction? Finally, let them explain
why, when Austria paused to "converse"
with Russia, he sent the Czar the ultimatum
which could mean only war. That he ordered
his troops to invade Belgium and France

before declaring war, would of itself discredit his pretended reverence for peace. It was the last link in the chain of hypocrisy, stretching back over twenty-five years.

Thus the Atrocious War began, and atrocious in history will be William who began it.

As we picture him watching his neighbors year after year and waiting till he judged the moment ripe for smiting them, we have a vision of a butcher who goes out every day to look over his cattle, and even hands them wisps of hay to make them believe that he is peaceable and friendly; and then the morning comes when he hurries them off to the shambles. Such is the rôle played by a War-Lord, drunk with ambition for world-dominion.[1]

---

[1] The first sources for the diplomacy which led up to the War are, of course, the Official Papers of the various belligerents. The best brief analysis of these is in *The Evidence in the Case*, by James M. Beck. (New York: Putnam, 1914.) An exhaustive treatise is that of Ellery C. Stowell: *The Diplomacy of the War of 1914*, vol. i. (Boston: Houghton Mifflin Co. 1915.)

CHAPTER X

BELGIUM

All pity choked with custom of fell deeds:
. . . .
That this foul deed shall smell above the earth
With carrion men, groaning for burial.
                    SHAKESPEARE: *Julius Cæsar*, III, I.

DURING the last days of July, 1914, seven and a half million Belgian men, women, and children lived their ordinary lives, industrious, peaceful, and thrifty people, little blazoned in the world's dispatches. A fortnight later, Belgium had suffered martyrdom which will keep her name and that of her destroyer alive as long as posterity shall remember examples of supreme heroism and of Satanic guilt. So nigh was grandeur to her dust, and so unsuspected by those in whom it dwelt!

During fourscore years Belgium had existed as an independent nation, coveted alike by France and Germany, but unharmed by both;

for her right to existence had been guaranteed by the great Powers. Even in 1870, when Prussia was hurling her armies against France, and the passage through Belgium would have been most useful, Bismarck showed sufficient regard for public opinion in Europe and America to declare that Prussia would not violate the neutrality of Belgium. Bismarck pricked any of the Ten Commandments like a bubble, when he thought he could gain anything thereby; but, being a statesman, he avoided wanton lawlessness, not because it was wanton, but because it was bad statecraft.

William II, however, who deemed himself greater than Bismarck, thought that he proved his superiority by violating all laws.

On the morning of August 4 he sent his troops into Belgium. That same afternoon, when Sir Edward Goschen interviewed the German Chancellor, in the forlorn hope that the avalanche of war already started might be checked mid-course, he found Bethmann-

Hollweg "very agitated." For England had announced that, if Belgium were invaded, she would fulfil her solemn promise to defend Belgian neutrality. "His Excellency," Goschen records, "at once began a harangue which lasted for about twenty minutes. He said that the step taken by the [British] Government was terrible to a degree; just for a word — 'neutrality,' a word which in war-time has so often been disregarded — *just for a scrap of paper*, Great Britain was going to make war on a kindred nation who desired nothing better than to be friends with her." [1] That "scrap of paper," torn by the command of the impatient Kaiser, will float for ages on every wind as an indictment of his crime.

On that same day, August 4, Bethmann-Hollweg made this explanation to the German Reichstag: —

Gentlemen, we are now in a state of necessity, and necessity knows no law! Our troops have occupied Luxemburg, and perhaps [as a matter

[1] Stowell, 1, 365.

of fact the speaker knew that Belgium had been invaded that morning] are already on Belgian soil. Gentlemen, that is contrary to the dictates of international law. It is true that the French Government has declared at Brussels that France is willing to respect the neutrality of Belgium as long as her opponent respects it. We knew, however, that France stood ready for the invasion. France could wait, but we could not wait. A French movement upon our flank upon the lower Rhine might have been disastrous. So we were compelled to override the just protest of the Luxemburg and Belgian Governments. The wrong — I speak openly — that we are committing, we will endeavor to make good as soon as our military goal has been reached. Anybody who is threatened, as we are threatened and is fighting for his highest possessions, can have only one thought — how he is to hack his way through! [1]

These words, blurted out by the Chancellor in palliation of Germany's crime, will be stamped as indelibly on the pages of history as was Belshazzar's condemnation on the wall of his banquet-room. Addressing the members

[1] Stowell, I, 445–46.

of the Reichstag, into whom the venom of
Kultur had penetrated, Bethmann-Hollweg
knew that his plea of necessity would be accepted as a matter of course: for the first principle of Kultur teaches that whatever Prussianized Germany wishes to do is therefore
"necessary." The burglar who, on being
caught, should protest that it was "necessary"
for him to break a bank, would be only a ready
disciple of German Kultur.

So the Kaiser's troops violated the Belgian
frontier, and advanced with clatter of cavalry
scouts and goose-step tramp of infantry, with
rumble of cannon and whirr of myriad motors
and trucks, into the doomed country. "Let
us through!" shouted the Prussians; "let us
through, or we will hack our way through!"
And although Belgium was but a small country — her army at its maximum counting less
than one to ten of the Germans — knowing
the awful risk, she resolutely and without fear
blocked the way. In the face of men for all
time she bore witness that she set honor above

life, and she showed that valor, being of the soul, bears no relation to bodily size.

At Liège she checked the onslaught of the Germans, who were at first surprised by her foolhardiness, and then infuriated. They quickly threw off the restraints of civilized warfare, in which they were never at ease, and proved themselves in acts the Huns they were at heart, if not by descent. Repulsed again and again from the forts of Liège, they had to wait until the mass of their troops came up, regiment after regiment, like the successive waves of a rising flood, with their monster siege-guns, the latest achievement of Krupp Kultur, before they could swamp the Belgian defenders and pass on their way westward.

Glorious Liège! Her name will shine beside that of Thermopylæ. Thrice fortunate the heroes who died there defending their homes, their country's honor, and civilization itself! As long as time shall be, their example shall hearten brave men to fight for liberty against desperate odds; and when this titanic struggle between the armies of Might and the armies of Right has closed, and the free nations of the world look back upon it, they will overflow with gratitude for Liège. Six or seven days are but a moment in a man's lifetime; and yet the six or seven days during which Liège blocked the onrush of the German hordes, outweigh in fatefulness many a century in the lifetime of civilization. They saved France; with France, they saved the cause of the Allies. That check shattered the military plan which Germany had been elaborating for forty years, the plan in which every minute detail was worked out, everything mechanical was provided for and under control. One thing alone had Krupp Kultur overlooked; it had assumed that the Belgians like the Germans were machines, not souls; but that small, brave company of Belgian souls at Liège rose up and dashed against and dislocated the gigantic German machine, and wrecked the mechanically perfect plan of Krupp Kultur. The Germans never entered

Paris. On the contrary, they were driven back from the Marne to the Aisne, and they would have retreated to the Rhine, if the French munitions had not given out. The heroes of Liège had not died in vain.

Enraged by the resistance, perhaps stung by the loathing with which the civilized world greeted their declaration that their most solemn promise was only a scrap of paper, the Germans proceeded to wreak on innocent Belgium their system of Frightfulness. The horrors they committed in those weeks of August and September cannot be put into words. To whatever town they came, though it were unfortified and undefended, they came as Huns into whose ruthless hands modern science had put tools of destruction unknown to their ancestors. Attila's barbarians spread fire from house to house by the torch; the barbarians of William II carried incendiary pastilles, which they threw into rooms, and engines filled with petroleum which they sprayed on the condemned buildings. Here they battered down by cannonade; there they blew up by dynamite. In the country, they demolished the tiny villages, where only old men and women and children lingered. And they did not spare even the solitary peasant's cottage. They looted first and then they laid waste. In the cities of Flanders and Brabant they made the masterpieces of the famous architects who built in a golden age their special butt, as if the mere sight of Beauty maddened them.

But it was upon living, human beings that German Frightfulness, formulated by the General Staff and sanctioned by Emperor William, vented itself without mercy. Scarcely a place escaped horror in one or many forms. Unarmed men, burgomasters and local notables, quiet shopkeepers, workmen and servants, were seized, maltreated, killed, some without warning, others after prolonged suspense, and the refinement of cruelty.

We read that the Kaiser's minions took a

father and son into a garden, shot the son,
compelled the father to stand at the feet of
the corpse, and then shot him. They compelled wives to look on while their husbands
were shot, before subjecting the women to
outrage worse than death. They had no pity
for children. In a single house they dispatched
a little girl and her two smaller brothers; and,
as if they were Herod's hirelings, they slaughtered even infants, skewering some on their
bayonets, ripping or slashing others with
their swords. Where they did not kill, they
mutilated. They resorted to the savage
practice of taking hostages, whom they slew
if any irresponsible inhabitant was unruly or
committed a violent act or was suspected of
sniping. Often they did not wait for a pretext; but sometimes, as at Louvain, their
soldiers fired into the streets from the natives' windows, and then, with the cry that
the Louvainers were sniping the Germans,
they redoubled their orgy of rape and pillage,
and arson and murder. Sometimes they led

out their victims in large batches and massacred them by forties and fifties and by hundreds. In one town they herded a crowd of men, women, and children into the marketplace, and opened fire upon them without warning; and we hear that three little boys, seeing their elders drop around them, clasped each other tightly and died together when the volley reached them. Once, at least, they ranged their victims in two parallel lines, those behind having to wait and behold those in front fall, some killed, others writhing in agony, before their own turn came. These thorough Huns did not overlook priests; having compelled one curé to help in digging a huge grave for a heap of slaughtered, they then shot him, there being left a hole large enough to roll his body into. Hellish was their conduct towards women — women? — towards females of any age. In one village a grandmother of eighty and a little girl of eight succumbed to the lust of William's soldiers. The officers are accused of reserving

the best for themselves. Nor did horrors stop
on the threshold of nunneries.[1]

These things, being a part of history, must
be recorded here. I cite at random only a
few examples, few, but typical. Whoever
will, can read the infernal roster, in which the
number of individual victims mounts to
thousands and still is incomplete. Such acts
link William II of Hohenzollern in the same
exorbitance of atrocity with Nana Sahib of
Cawnpore.

The War-Lord who permitted his army to
inflict these horrors upon the noncombatant
civilians of entire provinces cannot be expected to forbid his soldiers in the field to
drive women and children before them to
screen them in an attack: nor could he be
so squeamish as to feel ashamed when they
fired upon ambulances, or shelled hospital
ships.

[1] See the *Bryce Report*, and the statements issued by
Professor Joseph Bédier for the French investigating com-
mittee.

In modern war, even as it has been fought
by civilized nations, the brutal passions which
were once uppermost in all men, but which
in most men have been slowly subdued, burst
into fierce activity. Indeed, war, being a re-
version to a barbaric state, is the natural environment where these barbaric instincts flour-
ish. Rapine, murder, and pillage blacken the
annals of every campaign; but the Germans
who practiced them on the Belgians in 1914
were loaded with a special burden of guilt.
The apologist of Teuton ferocity cannot plead
that these fiendish acts were sporadic, or
were due to drunkenness, or to a sudden
explosion of fury, or to any other unpre-
meditated cause. In their system of war, the
Prussians not only foresaw but prescribed
their use. They knew that bloodthirstiness
and lust and the mania for destruction lie
very near the surface in soldiers, and they
touched off these passions as deliberately as
they exploded a mine. This they called
Frightfulness, and they thought that by

applying it in all its diabolical rigor they could terrorize the Belgians into abject submission. Their self-centred psychology misled them in this case as in many others. Are we to infer that *they* would have been terrorized by such atrocities? They never broke the Belgian spirit, and it was not until hundreds of thousands of their troops bestrode Belgium, that her gallant 'people ceased to resist.

Then it was that the modern Huns discovered that they had raised up against themselves a record of infamy which all their armies could not blot out, and which all the victories they might win, were it that world-dominion they coveted, could never condone. Human suffering speaks through dumb mouths which no tyrant can smother. The anguish and martyrdom suffered by the ravished Belgian women, by the innocent little children, by the unarmed men, old and young, horrified every humane heart the wide world round; and though the Prussian dynasty were to reign from now till Doomsday, on the brow of each Hohenzollern despot, as he mounts his throne, invisible hands will stamp the name "Belgium," as ineffaceable as the brand of Cain.

CHAPTER XI

MENDACITY

Of every malice that wins hate in Heaven,
Injury is the end; and all such end
Either by force or fraud afflicteth others.
But because fraud is man's peculiar vice,
More it displeases God; and so stand lowest
The fraudulent, and great dole assails them.

DANTE: *Hell*, XI, 22–27. (Longfellow's translation.)

NOT alone in Belgium did Prussian psychology err. Regarding the Belgians as so puny as to be negligible, and judging them as if they were Germans, it had taken it for granted that they would not oppose an empire whose army outnumbered theirs by ten to one; but the Belgians, reasoning and feeling in quite un-Prussian ways, dared to resist, and their resistance, as we have seen, although it was brief, threw out of joint the grand strategy of the German Staff. The Kaiser did not celebrate Napoleon's Birthday by a dinner in Paris, as he had planned, nor did he dictate overwhelming terms of peace to France. Neither did he paralyze Russia by a sudden drive.

German psychology, unhinged by Belgium's courage, was smashed beyond repair by England's decision. For England, instead of being the weary Titan, afraid of Suffragettes and terrified by Irish factions, instead of being a sordid money-bags concerned only in amassing wealth, declared that she would fulfil her pledge and defend Belgium. She, at least, would not subscribe to the Prussian doctrine that small nations had no right to exist; and although she had only "a gentleman's agreement" with France, that to her was binding.

At the first suspicion that England's psychology would not function as the Prussians had calculated, the German Chancellor tried to seduce her to desert France and Belgium. In the German code, honor pledged in the past is to be thrown over, if it prove inconvenient in the present. To Bethmann-Hollweg this was so self-evident a truth that he listened with incredulity and then flew into wild rage when he was told that England did not look upon a solemn compact as "a mere scrap of paper." The next day, when the British Prime Minister told the Commons and the world that no Englishman could listen to this "infamous proposal," his laconic statement required no amplification. Everywhere outside of Germany it was held to be obvious that he could make no other.

Then burst upon England the wrath of Kaiser and Chancellor, and of every German who spoke out; and tiny boys and girls were taught like parrots to repeat the curse, "*Gott strafe England*," — God punish England,— and to glower with hate whenever they heard England's name. So a robber, who is surprised by a policeman just as he is in the act of sandbagging a victim, turns with fury upon the policeman, curses him and calls him unfair and the despoiler of the ancient profession of robbers — the profession by which the Hohenzollerns had thriven for centuries.

The frenzy into which Germany flew over England's keeping her promise to defend Belgium and the rights of small nations, became chronic. It was a confession that she was the ultimate enemy at whom the vast German war preparations were aimed. The official pretext alleged was that Germany took up arms to save herself and the civilization of Western Europe from the Slavic Peril. We were asked to believe that the subjects of the Hohenzollern and the Hapsburg Emperors lived in dread of being submerged by a flood of Muscovite barbarians, which would sweep away Kultur and the inferior but still recognized civilization of England, France, and Italy. The Czar's mobilization of part of his army to succor Serbia, after Austria had not only mobilized her troops, but was actually bombarding the Serbian capital, was advanced by the Germans as a sign that the floodgates of the Slavic Peril had broken down. Instead of making straight for Russia, however, the German armies made straight for

Belgium and France — a strange blunder in geography for a people whose impeccable maps were drawn by Kiepert and whose wonderful guide-books were compiled by Baedeker! Only a commander-in-chief saturated with the logic of Kultur would rush due west to repel a foe who was massing his forces to attack four hundred miles due east.

In truth, the Kaiser was simply carrying out the plan laid down years before by the General Staff: in spite of England's interference, he still hoped to crush France before English help could reach her. This accomplished, he counted on being able to ward off an English descent on the French coast, if one were attempted, — which seemed unlikely, — and to detach the larger part of his Western troops for service against Russia. A desperate hope, quickly blasted by Sir John French's masterly retreat and General Joffre's victorious strategy. One morning the Kaiser's scouts looked gloatingly down on Paris from the terrace at Saint-Germain, as on a treasure which they had only to stretch out their hand to grasp; the next day those scouts and all the Kaiser's corps were hurrying back from the Marne to the Aisne. William had the satisfaction of sneering at "England's contemptible little army"; but Sir John French might well ask: "If eighty thousand English soldiers sufficed to check eight hundred thousand Germans, is 'contemptible' the fittest word to apply to them?"

From that time on, the Germans have never disguised the fact that they regarded England as their chief adversary, whom they vowed to destruction. More than once, the Kaiser strove to inveigle France and Russia, either singly or together, to make a separate peace, which would allow him to deal with England alone; but both Russia and France held true to their compact. The German wrath against England was no sudden outbreak of hysteria in which one utters vain ravings; it was deliberately stimulated and fostered and passed on.

Lissauer popularized it in a "Hymn of Hate," to be sung by civilians at their gatherings and by soldiers on the march or in the trenches; and the Kaiser decorated Lissauer for this addition to the hymnal of Kultur. Journalists, politicians, bureaucrats, professors, retired army officers, vied with each other in hurling invectives against the English. They even stooped to borrow some of Napoleon's taunts — "perfidious Albion," "nation of shopkeepers": and this was not unnatural, because the Kaiser had unwittingly involved himself in those British toils which had slowly strangled and slain Napoleon.

If Kultur did not distort the vision of its possessors whenever they look away from the mirror which reflects themselves, the Kaiser might have meditated on certain historic coincidences. At the end of the sixteenth century, it was England, a small and not populous country, which shattered the world-empire of Spain. A hundred years later, when Louis XIV lorded it over half of Europe, it was again England who shattered the power of France. Another century passed and England, the head of the European coalition, which but for her would have dissolved ingloriously, smote Napoleon, whose empire stretched from the Dnieper to Cadiz. History may not repeat itself in William's Atrocious War of 1914; and yet a historian cannot fail to perceive that England is for the fourth time championing Liberty against a would-be world-despot. Hitherto the stars in their courses have fought for her.

Very quickly the Prussian mask fell. It was not French Revenge, not the Slavic Peril, against which William made war, it was England. *Delenda est Britannia!* — Britain must be wiped out! — that was the inspiration of the long years of military preparation, of the creation of a great German Navy, of the toast to "The Day," of the truculence of the German reptile press and of the Kaiser's amiable references to peace. He had not intended, however, to attack England until he had dis-

posed of France and Russia; but his own
bungling diplomacy ruined his scheme. Bismarck always arranged it so as to fight only
one enemy at a time: but William, knowing
better than Bismarck the rules of statecraft,
waited until all his enemies would unite to
take the field against him before he declared
war on one of them.

Nothing comparable to the frenzied out-
cries of the Germans, when they found that
they had leaped in the dark into a world-war,
has been heard in modern times. They raged
at England's "betrayal," berating her for not
telling them that she would keep her pledge
to Belgium, a rage which I have likened to
that of a footpad who is interrupted by the
appearance of a policeman.

More interesting, however, were the ex-
pressions of utter amazement which the Germans sent up on perceiving that civilized
people everywhere abhorred the German violation of Belgium and the sequent atrocities.
Their amazement, at least, was genuine; it

is an electric torch by which we can explore the labyrinth of Kultur. They did not, they could not understand how any foreigner could be so foolish as to suppose that a treaty was more than a scrap of paper, if its observance incommoded Germany.

Among many manifestations of this surprise none equaled the address issued early in October, 1914, by the Ninety-three Intellectuals. "As heralds of truth" these men, who had enjoyed a reputation as pillars of German scholarship, spoke the words they were bidden to speak. Here are the heads of their denials: —

It is not true that Germany is guilty of having caused this war. Neither the people, the Government, nor the Kaiser, wanted war. Germany did her utmost to prevent it; for this assertion the world has documentary proof. . . .

It is not true that we trespassed in neutral Belgium. It has been proved that France and England had resolved on such a trespass, and it has likewise been proved that Belgium had agreed to their doing so. . . .

It is not true that the life and property of a

single Belgian citizen was injured by our soldiers without the bitterest self-defense having made it necessary. . . .

It is not true that our troops treated Louvain brutally. Furious inhabitants having fallen upon them treacherously in their quarters, our troops, with aching hearts, were obliged to fire a part of the town as a punishment. . . .

It is not true that our warfare pays no respect to international laws. It knows no undisciplined cruelty. . . .

It is not true that the combat against our so-called Militarism is not a combat against our civilization [Kultur], as our enemies hypocritically pretend it is. Were it not for German Militarism, German Civilization [Kultur] would long since have been extirpated. . . .

We shall search in vain for any counterpart to this manifesto, which proved, as nothing else could prove, the complete subservience of the German university professors to the Kaiser and his Ring. The Government cracked the whip, and the Ninety-three fell into line, clicked their heels together, saluted, and repeated their formulas. Not in our generation will German scholarship recover its prestige after such an exhibition. We were told that German scholars were impersonal, impartial, objective seekers for truth — whether that truth were in science or in religion or in the humanities. What becomes of that boast when Harnack and Haeckel and Ostwald and Eduard Meyer sign such a paper as this, containing statements not only unverified but unverifiable, not only doubtful but false? What credence will non-Germans give hereafter to Harnack and the Ninety-three when they discourse on their specialties? If Harnack could sign his name to the denial, "*It is not true* that we trespassed in neutral Belgium," how can we trust his assertions in the Higher Criticism? When we turn back to the works which brought these men distinction, we shall see the shadow of suspicion on every page: for we shall remember that the mind which produced them was of such nature — call it essentially unscientific or untruthful — that it adopted eagerly the false statements of the Address.

Incidentally, the Ninety-three confirm two facts which many German apologists try to evade: first, that, but for German Militarism, German Kultur "would long since have been extirpated"; and, secondly, that German warfare "knows no *undisciplined* cruelty." The cruelty it practices is premeditated, disciplined — in a word, Frightfulness.

Kultur was, as I have said, a process of breeding in and in. It created a truly wonderful efficiency among Germans in Germany; but, being based on egotism, it rendered them less and less capable of understanding other races; and this incapacity increased until they made no pretense of understanding them. They assumed that, as non-German peoples were inferior, their "psychology" did not matter.

Germany's decision to violate Belgium dated from many years back. She constructed a mesh of railroads to the Belgian frontiers, massed troops and supplies there, took it to be axiomatic that her armies would cross

there — a "necessity," as Bethmann-Hollweg baldly declared. Accordingly, her amazement was unfeigned when in her egomania
she made the discovery that the rest of the
world had not been assuming that Teutonic
plans and ambitions, and those alone, should
monopolize the attention of mankind. She
was as much astonished that foreigners should
be shocked by her violation of treaties and
by her damnably deliberate application of
Frightfulness, as Australian cannibals would
be to learn that cannibalism was abhorrent
to civilized men. The naïveté of her aston-
ishment measures the insoluble residue of
barbarism in the German nature — even in
the Ninety-three Intellectuals.

"The Prussian," Goethe is reported to
have said, "is cruel by birth; civilization will
make him ferocious." Goethe was not a
Prussian, but he will be hailed as a prophet,
if in the far retrospect the ferocity which the
Prussianized Germans have displayed in the
Atrocious War shall prove to be the inevi-

table reaction of Civilization on Kultur. The champions of Kultur, who had been telling each other that they were the greatest beings in the world, who have even invented a new class of mammals, Supermen, to which they alone belonged, were maddened when Civilization, which they discarded, dared to plant itself in the path of Kultur.

Besides cruelty, the Prussians possessed in a superlative degree another barbaric trait. The late Charles Francis Adams, writing a few days before his death in March, 1915, criticizing the plea of German apologists that Americans did not understand because they could not "think like Germans," said: —

Suspecting this in my own case, I have of late confined my reading on this topic almost exclusively to German sources. I have been taking a course in Nietzsche and Treitschke, as also in the German "Denkschrift," illumined by excerpts from the German papers in this country and the official utterances of Chancellor von Bethmann-Hollweg. The result has been most disastrous. It has utterly destroyed my capacity for judicial consideration. I can only say that

if what I find in those sources is the capacity
to think Germanically, I would rather cease
thinking at all. It is the absolute negation of
everything which in the past tended to the ele-
vation of mankind, and the installation in place
thereof of a system of thorough dishonesty,
emphasized by brutal stupidity. There is a low
cunning about it, too, which is to me in the last
degree repulsive.

Low Cunning — that is the twin of Cruelty
in the Prussianized German nature. There is
a cunning — that of the politicians of the
Renaissance, for instance, or that generated
by ecclesiasticism — which implies that its
adepts have passed over the crest of civilization and are sinking into decline. Their souls
being dead, they go on living by their wits.
Instead of wisdom they practice worldly
wisdom. It is diamond cut diamond among
them.

In contrast with this civilized cunning
stands that of the savage or the barbarian.
We know it by its crudeness, its naïveté, its
inherent inefficiency. The barbarian who re-

sorts to it half suspects that it does not fool his enemy; but he cannot discover why it fails, and he lacks skill or sophistication to devise something subtle that will work. The German nature has never been subtle, and Kultur, by reducing the Prussianized Germans to a condition of self-centred isolation, in which they could not penetrate the motives and ideals of other races, limited them to a barbarian cunning. To the weak and timid, lying serves as a sort of protective coloration. But the Prussianized Germans, with eight million soldiers under arms, were neither, and they employed mendacity bluntly as a weapon for overcoming neutrals whom they could not bombard into silence or asphyxiate by poisonous gases. To devise a thoroughly successful lie, however, calls for talent of a very different order from that which fabricates Krupp's howitzers.

The parent German lie from which the others sprang was, as we have seen, the declaration that the Allies attacked Germany intending to destroy her, and so forced her to act on the defensive, as she was notoriously opposed to war. What is the truth as the documents have shown it? It is, first, that Austria mobilized her army against Serbia before Russia began to mobilize her Southeastern Army Corps; next, that Germany threatened Russia with war unless she demobilized; thirdly, that the Czar pledged himself to commit no hostile act until time should be allowed for a conference of the Powers on the Austro-Serb quarrel; but, finally, that the German Emperor refused to consent to any delay, and declared war on Russia.

Even more monstrous is the German assertion that the Western Powers were the aggressors. A nation which premeditates war on a neighbor makes ready before it strikes. France in July, 1914, was not only unprepared to attack Germany, but to defend herself against attack. If, as the Germans allege, she had agreed with Belgium to make a sudden invasion into Germany, how did it hap-

pen that, when the German thunderbolt fell,
France had no troops in place to give Belgium
immediate succor? How did it happen that,
on the contrary, French troops were so backward that they could not come up in time
to give really valid assistance before Eastern
Belgium was lost? In Lorraine and in the
Vosges — where large bodies of French troops
were always stationed — they did check the
German onslaught; but when they needed
reserves, they had to wait for them during
terribly critical days — waiting which would
not have been necessary if the French Army
had been prepared. A nation which *starts* a
vast aggressive war without looking to its
supply of ammunition is crazy. The supply
of the French gave out within a month, and
they were thereby prevented from forcing
the Germans, who were in full retreat from
the Marne, straight back to their frontier.
This lack it was which enabled the Germans
to entrench along the Aisne and in the Ar-
gonne. The pretense that the French armies

were straining at the leash to attack Germany is utterly false. An aggressor who counts on surprising his antagonist does not withdraw his army six miles behind his own frontier and wait for the antagonist to begin. France did that in the vain hope of preserving peace.

Still more preposterous is the German insinuation that England was the ringleader of the Allies in their plot to overthrow Germany. For some five centuries at least the English have been proficient in figures, and we may safely affirm that, in all their computations, they have never discovered that one hundred and sixty thousand equal eight millions. Yet that was the disproportion between the immediately available English troops and the German, when Emperor William entered upon his specious "aggressive-defensive" war. True, the British Navy had just completed its annual manœuvres, but these were no more intended as a threat against Germany than the annual field exercises of the German Army had been a direct challenge to Russia or to France. In his wildest fit of megalomania, John Bull would never have boasted that one British soldier was a match for fifty Germans; and yet this is what the Germans attribute to him when they allege that he forced the struggle upon them.

The sequence of events which we have traced shows that England actually waited until the Germans had invaded Belgium and France before deciding to fight, and that then her preparations for sending troops across the Channel were so inadequate that her expedition could not check the Germans in Belgium and reached France only in time to take part in the great retreat. The Kaiser correctly described her eighty thousand mèn on the Continent as a "contemptible little army," for he reckoned by millions. These facts dispose of the charge that England either made or planned an aggressive war against Germany. Even her mighty Navy did not at once take the offensive.

German mendacity has exhausted its ingenuity in inventing pretexts for the violation of Belgium. Of these the most characteristic is that, as Belgium was about to attack Germany, Germany was forced in self-defense to attack her first. This is as if a giant ruffian, bent on killing and robbing a neighbor, should start to cross an intervening lot, and the owner of that lot, a frail young woman, should refuse him passage, whereupon he outraged her, and went on his murderous way. And when people cried out in horror at his brutality, he retorted that he acted in self-defense, as the frail young woman was about to outrage him. German apologists for the devastation of Belgium illustrate what I mean when I say that German mendacity bears witness to the insoluble barbaric residue in the German nature. Bethmann-Hollweg's first avowal that "necessity" forced them to invade Belgium, and that it was wrong, cannot be explained away. The future student who tabulates the score or more of "justifications," some official, some private, all mutually contradictory, which German defenders have since devised, will assemble an unparalleled exhibit of abortive casuistry.

I leave unnoticed the mendacity manufactured for home consumption by the official organs. That is a form of deception practiced by all governments in war-time, and it seems to succeed in proportion to the inability of the people to think for themselves. What shall we infer as to the intelligence of German troops who were told on reaching Brussels that they were in Paris? How shall we estimate the credulity of the German public which was informed that the Kaiser and his Army had taken Paris, but had refused to enter it in order to escape the typhus fever and cholera which raged there? In any other country but Germany we should suspect that the official purveyors of mendacity rated their countrymen's gullibility very high.

CHAPTER XII

THE PLOT TO GERMANIZE AMERICA

A Countryman returning home one winter's day, found a Snake by the hedge-side, half dead with cold. Taking compassion on the creature, he laid it in his bosom and brought it home to his fireside to revive it. No sooner had the warmth restored it, than it began to attack the children of the cottage. Upon this the Countryman, whose compassion had saved its life, took up a mattock and laid the Snake dead at his feet. — Those who return evil for good, may expect their neighbor's pity to be worn out at last.

Æsop's Fables.

WE Americans have other means by which to treat German proficiency in the art of deception; for when we raised a cry of indignation over the "scrap of paper" crime, and then a cry of horror over the atrocities in Belgium, the German Government dispatched to this country a squad of apologists and plotters, who, in collusion with Germans already here, conducted such a campaign as has never been seen before — a campaign which on its criminal side would not have been tolerated by an Administration which had possessed either courage or regard for American honor. Only once before in the history of this Republic had its President stood by while those who were plotting its subversion worked unchecked; that President was James Buchanan.

It soon became evident that the German propagandists were plotting for something much more tangible than America's "moral" sympathy. They addressed us first in the tone of one whose feelings have been hurt by the unexpected coolness of a "dear friend"; but when they found that their explanations did not move us, they resumed their natural Prussian voice, rough, truculent, and defiant. They told us that we were not a nation, but a mob, at the mercy of the mob spirit, which was then controlled by British lies. They warned us that William II would lose no time in punishing us after he had vanquished the Allies. They argued very little, supposing that unsupported assertions or flat denials were more effective. They resorted freely to their characteristic method of attributing to others baseness which they themselves practiced. The hirelings of their reptile press, for instance, charged the great American newspapers with being controlled by "British gold," and the subsidized spokesmen of the Kaiser insinuated that our public leaders were under British influence.

Even in that crisis, involving the future of civilized man on this earth, one could not help smiling at the ludicrous efforts of the Prussianized spellbinders to coax the Americans to their cause. They repelled the charge that Germany had rather a scant allowance of freedom, by asserting that, on the contrary, the Germans exercised a much ampler elective right than did the British or the Americans. The Kaiser, they declared, instead of being an autocrat, enjoyed less authority than the President of the United States. The charge that Militarism dominated the Fatherland was a calumny; nothing more Democratic could be imagined than the German military system. Equally baseless were hostile references to Junkerism: there had been a time when perhaps the Junkers exerted a trifling influence on Prussia, but, like the dodo, the Junker was now an extinct species.

Equally false, maliciously false, was the impression common in America that the Hohenzollern had been an ambitious dynasty, warlike, cruel towards victims too weak to defend themselves, perfidious, and unscrupulous. Most diligent were the Kaiser's paid apologists in drawing a portrait of him that would fascinate Americans. They glossed over his bellicose speeches; they interpreted his fondness for rattling the scabbard as playfulness. A hater of England, he? Why, he wore English tennis flannels, and prided himself on equaling the English at yachting. As we followed their descriptions of him, his glistening helmet and military uniform, and sword and spurs, and even his boar's-tush mustaches dropped away, and he stood there in a gray Quaker suit and broad-brimmed hat, the reincarnation of William Penn, with the conventional smile playing round his lips.

Such propaganda could originate only in minds which took it for granted that Americans of intelligence — if there were any — knew nothing about German history, politics, or conditions, and that all other Americans believed what they were told, just as if they were Germans. The propagandists dimly perceived that the methods, which worked to perfection at home, were ineffectual here; but instead of changing their tactics, they continued to use them with redoubled vigor. Their motto was: "If a bad lie does not succeed, reinforce it by a worse."

Dr. Dernburg, whose aptitudes commended him to the Kaiser, came over as the special Imperial envoy to cajole the Americans; and for half a year the competition between him and Ambassador Bernstorff at

Washington produced utterances hitherto unmatched on this side of the water. Dr. Dernburg's forte lay in misquoting or in garbling documents, which he would then discuss with an assumed judicial air, and draw from their mutilated remains conclusions opposite from those which their authors intended. And when his ruse was exposed,[1] he went on brazenly repeating it, as if he were confident that those who listened to him had no flair for truth. Where he did not falsify, as in his quotations from Gladstone, he spun specious arguments like those against British Navalism, or those intended to justify German violations of law and humanity. To his highly Kultured moral sense, the *Lusitania* massacre brought reassuring proof that Gott still blessed the Teutonic enterprise. Ambassador Bernstorff's exploits need not be rehearsed here. It is only fair, however, to

[1] See the exposure of him in the *New York Sunday Times* by Miss Agnes Repplier and Dr. J. W. White. Reprinted as a pamphlet.

quote from an interview which he gave to the press on August 31, 1914 — mark the date:—

1. The war is won. The coalition has been defeated in Western Europe. German defeat on land is now out of the question.

2. The aims of the German General Staff have been attained. The Allies have been so badly and so suddenly worsted that Germany is free to withdraw, as she has begun to do, great numbers of men to ward off the Russian invasion.[1]

Many other accredited agents of the Kaiser would deserve mention in a thorough study of the apostles of Kultur in America, men chosen because they best represented their Imperial master; but I pass over here the experts of the "reptile press," the renegade Jews, the paid hack-writers, the official bureaucrats and spies, and mention only the professors. Some of these had been planted in the United States a good while before; others were sent over to do special work. A world-authority on the altruistic emotions

[1] *Boston Herald*, September 1, 1914.

of the caterpillar, let us say, would pull the wires to be invited to lecture at one of our universities; and when he addressed his American audience, hungry for entomological information, he cruelly abandoned the caterpillar and poured forth a pro-German appeal. The crudeness of this trick also suggests the barbarian, and its employer doubtless wondered why he could not keep on fooling Americans with so primitive a device. But there were professors of other kinds. One expounded the ethics of Kultur; another was sly and casuistical; a third frankly berated Americans. There were even spurious professors and shady missionaries of Prussianism who for excellent reasons adopted aliases.

Before this campaign had been long under way, it became evident that the Kaiser's agents had a double purpose. They worked not only to propitiate American public opinion, in the hope that it would voluntarily espouse the German cause, but also to organize the German-Americans in this country into a compact political party, which should terrorize, if it could not persuade the Government to aid Germany by direct or indirect means. As time went on, these conpirators grew brazen. They held meetings at which they openly preached sedition, and through the press they announced that they and the Irish-Americans would seize control of the country and rule it for the benefit of the Hohenzollern dynasty. Some of the most exuberant of them seem to have had a vision of a German Imperial Prince, sitting in the White House as Viceroy of the Kaiser.

Few flights of the imagination could be more comical than that which suggests that the Irish-Americans should unite with the Germans in a league to be dominated by the Germans. The Irish, who have often declared the somewhat slack rule of the English in Ireland too exasperating to be borne, would hardly find the strait-jacket régime of Prussia comfortable: and with their native talent for politics, which has given them power, local and national, out of all proportion to their numbers, they are not likely to abdicate in favor of the German-Americans, who have shown comparatively little ability as practical politicians. The Germans in Tammany Hall are controlled by the Irish; and that will be the relative position of the two races whatever be the terms of their alliance. German conspirators here, who flatter themselves that the Irish will sacrifice their position in America in order to promote the ambition of a Prussian or any other monarch in Europe, are hopelessly dense, and at the end of the bargain they will perceive that the Irish have exploited them for their own purposes here. The Irish intend to remain Americans.

The Kaiser's agents did not stop at openly preaching sedition. They spread secretly a network of violence such as has never before been attempted by aliens in a foreign country — a conspiracy all the more monstrous because Germany was officially at peace with the United States and pretended to desire American good-will. Acting under instructions which were traced to German and Austrian officials, the Teutonic miscreants placed bombs on outgoing steamers, blew up munitions factories, resorted to the intimidation of capitalists, organized strikes and *sabotage*, tried to wreck railroads, and made this country a base for hostile operations against the Allies with whom we were at peace.

For effrontery these proceedings have had no precedent here. Reverse the positions of the nations, and suppose that Americans, being engaged in a war with England, should carry on a similar campaign of mendacity and crime inside Germany, which was neutral. The German Government would suppress such conspirators within a week, and it would give short shrift to gentlemen who announced that they were going to take possession of Germany and to run it thereafter as an American province. In the United States, even sedition is allowed free speech; but, if the

Administration at Washington had not been both supine and self-seeking, it would have acted so decisively that the Teutonic conspirators would have been promptly checked. It remained for President Wilson to announce to Congress that as a result of fifteen months' non-interference on his part there had grown up a formidable body of sedition, composed of persons whom he omitted to designate.

Examples abound of the low cunning in which Germans put their trust. When they perceived that their direct assault on American public opinion made no headway, they discarded the hyphen and the name "German," and formed organizations to uphold "American" truth, "American" interests, "American" national ideals, or "American" neutrality; so rogues ply their trade under assumed names.

Two manifestations of Kulturized craft ought not to be passed over. When the British blockade succeeded in cutting off most of Germany's food supplies by sea, the Teutons set up a whimper over the cruelty of starving to death the women and children of an entire nation. Coming from them, whose home government, after wrecking Belgium, left the Belgians to starve, this plea for humanity was peculiarly indecent. Hohenzollern Frightfulness towards the Belgians caused humane persons throughout the world to contribute at the rate of fifty million dollars a year to clothe and feed those victims for whose maintenance the Germans themselves were responsible. What part of the supplies the Germans diverted, we shall probably never know; but we see how they used the desperate sufferings of the Belgians as a device for saving four or five million dollars a month for the benefit of their own Army. The whimper of the Kaiser's agents in the United States was all the more nauseating, because at the very time when we were besought to relieve the women and children of Germany from famine, the German Chancellor and other high spokesmen of the Empire kept declaring that there was a superabundance of food, and that Germany could never be starved out. Who lied?

During the American Civil War, while the Union forces were slowly exhausting the Confederacy by constriction, there was no talk of allowing the British or French to send food to the Southern women and children; and in 1870, after the Prussians, having hemmed in Paris, proceeded to starve it out, they would have guffawed at the suggestion that they should let supplies for the famished Parisians pass. They knew that every hungry mouth diminished the dwindling store of provisions, and that every empty stomach lessened the power of resistance. But when the tables were turned, if they were turned, — and we have the Chancellor's word for it, that there was no lack of food, — the Germans whined that *they* must be spared the effects of a blockade, although they themselves and all other Western nations had used blockades as a legitimate form of warfare.

Similarly hypocritical was their campaign against the shipment of munitions to the Allies. The right of the merchants of a neutral country to sell goods to belligerents was recognized long ago in international law. The Germans have always exercised it; impartially, too, if it be true that they sold guns and munitions to both Russia and Japan in the war of 1904–05. Just before the outbreak of the Atrocious War, they were sending shiploads of arms to the Mexican revolutionists, who, they hoped, would involve us in their struggle and so prevent us from interfering in Europe. With equal impartiality they sold their wares to Turks and to some of the Balkan Christians up to 1912. Krupp's agents never inquired into the race, creed, or politics of a good customer. If the Kaiser himself was a stockholder in the Krupp Company, he had no reason to be dissatisfied with the dividends it paid him; but when, through his inability to keep a single ship, naval or mercantile, on the sea, he could not transport American munitions to Germany, his lobby at Washington and his agents throughout the United States started an agitation for an embargo. These conspirators found a certain number of disloyal public men in Congress, and sentimentalists who mistake the shadow for the substance and love to be duped, to join them in an attempt which, if it were successful, would violate American neutrality, flout international law, and be an admission that a foreign monarch controls the lawmaking of this nation.

Germany practiced a peculiarly ignoble form of deceit in permitting her subjects who came to this country to become naturalized American citizens, with the tacit understanding that, when they returned home, they might resume their German citizenship. The purpose of this double shuffle was evident as soon as the war broke out. Germans who had resided here for years, never hinting that they wished to become Americans, suddenly applied for naturalization papers, and were soon presiding at pro-German meetings or editing pro-German journals, and setting themselves up as expounders of the Americanism of Washington and Lincoln. One hardly knows which to despise more, the deceit or the impudence.

The final revelation as to Prussianized Germany came when the world realized the almost limitless extension of the German spy system. The spy, as trained and employed by Germany, is the meanest of creatures. It would be a libel on the microbes of an infectious disease to compare him to them. They do their work as all inanimate matter does; but he is a sentient being with a perverted will, who simulates the truth which his heart is incapable of feeling, and dissimulates the falsehood which is his second nature, in order to prepare the ruin of the unsuspecting persons among whom he glides. The German Government kept spies in every court; it planted them in foreign corporations; it used them to trail the intentions of other governments and of politicians; it insinuated them into laboratories and mills. They intrigued in Egypt and in India and in South Africa to foment risings against the English; they influenced the Japanese against America; they laid the train in Mexico for an explosion against this country; their burrowing in the Far East is known. Other nations — Russia, for instance, and Austria — have practiced espionage for centuries, but never on such a scale or with such diabolical cynicism or with such precision. Neither has any other nation found it so easy to persuade those of its citizens who settled abroad to consent to serve as non-commissioned supporters of the system. The Germans who for business or pleasure resided in Eastern France or in Paris; the German colonists who filtered into Western Poland; those who overran Italy and England, and their counterparts everywhere, had among them many who played with equal ease the rôles of propagandist and of spy. German missionaries, sent out to teach the heathen the religion of Gott, are ready agents of the German Secret Service Bureau.

In these various shapes Mendacity, which seems to be an indestructible element of the German nature, displays itself. The ominous fact is not that some Germans should lie or deceive or accept the spies' loathsome commissions — the wicked and the vile are found in every race; the ominous fact is, not only that the Prussianized German Government, having elaborated Mendacity as carefully as they perfected their Militarism, should find multitudes eager to practice it, but also that the German people, north, south, east, and west, should regard it as the most natural thing in life.

Is it not significant that Goethe, who was as far removed as possible from Prussian ideals, should embody in Mephistopheles — the Spirit of Falseness — this deep-seated national characteristic? The substance of his Mephistopheles was Pan-German and might be supplied today by the Kaiser and his

Ring; but Goethe himself supplied the keen edge and devilish sarcasm which make Mephistopheles the one unapproached creation in German dramatic literature.

Cruelty and Cunning — those are the ends to which Kultur logically leads: and of these the more hideous is Cunning. Cruelty denies the human bond which links every man to the race; but Cunning, Mendacity, denies Truth itself. Cruelty may burst out in an excess of passion and may be expiated by remorse, so far as there is any expiation for guilt whose victims perish. But Cunning is premeditated, merciless, too hardened to be capable of remorse. Dante, the terrible appraiser of guilt, reserved the lowest depths of hell for the Fraudulent — those who by Mendacity betrayed their fellow men.

That these conspirators have acted in ruthless disregard of the many Germans in the United States who abhor Prussianism and wish to stand loyally by this country and its institutions, was to be expected; for every

German in America who prefers America to Germany is a refutation of the claims of Dr. Dernburg and all the other propagandists of Kultur. Quite naturally, these victims of persecution and intimidation have kept silent; no census has been made of them; and the seditious have not hesitated to assert that *all* German-Americans are behind their conspiracy. When the "show-down" comes, there will be a tragic surprise for those who have been banking on the disloyalty of any large number of persons in the United States.

But Kultur employs a logic of its own, which results in what to non-Germans are contradictions stupefyingly bizarre. I have given two or three specimens of these already, but there is another which the student of Teutonic psychology ought not to overlook.

For a dozen years past the zealots of Kultur have told us that Germany surpasses other countries, not only in its powerful military organization, but in every walk of life. Every German is instructed precisely what he must do, and he does it thoroughly. The Government directs both his labors and his pleasures; it saves him in a thousand cases from the necessity of deciding for himself; it leaves nothing or almost nothing to his individual initiative; it watches over every class, and each unit in every class; it banishes poverty; it assures Germans of a stipend in their old age; it allows them to explore vast labyrinths of erudition; it offers them books, music, art, in heaping measure: and in return for all this, it exacts only obedience, that virtue from exercising which a German is supposed to derive as much pleasure as other persons derive from love. So Germany is, on the avowal of its own officials, the Earthly Paradise, dreamt of for ages and yearned for by sorely tried men and women of all races, and now at last put into happy operation by the wizards of Kultur.

But what strange fact is this which shatters our alluring vision of the Earthly Paradise? Why is it that emigrants east and west, north and south, discontented or downtrodden at home, do not flock thither in their search of happier conditions? Norwegians, Swedes, and Finns need only to cross the Baltic in order to reach the Happy Land; but instead, they voyage over the sundering Atlantic to the United States. One would imagine that the magnetic attraction would be so strong on Danes and Dutchmen that they would wipe out their frontiers and beg to be merged in the German Eden. Why are the Italians, rather a quick-witted people, so dull as to travel to America, where too often grinding toil and a precarious existence await them, when a day's journey would bring them into the Kaiser's Empire? And so of Slavs and Bulgars and Greeks and Syrians and Armenians, of Letts also and Magyars and mishandled Jews everywhere — why do not they lay down their burdens and become residents of this Prussianized Utopia?

More than twoscore years ago, in the kindness of their hearts the Germans insisted that the inhabitants of Alsace and Lorraine should share German hospitality. They argued that these people, having once been German, must quickly feel at home, like exiles after a long absence. Why is it, then, that they remain French, loathing everything German, refusing to see in the treatment they have had, or in the German ideals behind that treatment, the slightest resemblance to Paradise? Must we conclude that this German Happy Land is happy only for the Germans themselves, as the wasp's nest, made with much delicate precision and such perfect efficiency, is home only to wasps? And what is this dark fact, attested every year by the statisticians? The number of child suicides in Germany far exceeds, *per capita*, that in any other country. The Kingdom of Heaven is peopled with children. Can it be that a brief experience reveals to German children that Germany is not Heaven?

What becomes of Kultur as a universal system, if this be true? And what shall we say of the Kaiser's propagandists in the United States, who openly proclaim that they mean to Germanize this nation? Can we suppose that the millions of descendants of those who founded this country on principles which are the negation of Prussian Kultur, will abjure their faith? Or that the other millions who fled from Continental Europe to enjoy here opportunities and institutions denied them there, will meekly consent to live under German domination? Will the Germans themselves who have settled here and prospered and stubbornly refused to go home to the Fatherland, masquerading as Utopia — will they join in the conspiracy to destroy this Republic to which they or their fathers voluntarily escaped as to a place of salvation? The paid agents of the Kaiser we understand, but we believe that they do not represent the great body of the German immigration.

A child of ordinary intelligence could hardly fail to ask, after being told of the perfection of Germany and the irresistible attraction of the Fatherland for Germans, Why is it that the Germans do not go home and stay? Many of them have grown rich in this country, and they would be able to secure luxury in Germany, where wealth is not less potent than it is here; but neither rich nor poor go back. Is it from pure altruism that they, who cannot be enticed to return to Germany for good, insist that we and the rest of mankind must be Germanized? And is honor or logic wanting in those professors, who, having managed to slide into American university chairs and even to become naturalized citizens, make it their business to depreciate and actually to condemn everything American and to hold up everything German as a model for us to follow? Why do not they go home?

The paid propagandists of Germany, and her other enthusiastic emigrants in foreign lands, remind us of those suspiciously pious persons who protest at all times that they yearn to go to heaven at once, but take every possible precaution to live on earth as long as they can.

World-power or downfall! That is the German motto in the Atrocious War. With what desperation the Kaiser has been seeking victory appears, not less in his cynical disregard of solemn treaties and in the ferocity of his devastation of Belgium, than in the campaign of crime carried on by agents in this country. Only men convinced that they must win, at any cost and by any means, could resort to the terrorist methods which these agents use. But what if the Kaiser does not win? In what state will the hyphenate, seditious Germans here be left? Can they suppose that the Americans, who are and intend to remain Americans, will welcome them as neighbors? Will the American workmen who have been thrown out of employment by the blowing-up of their factories feel kindly towards the Teutons who committed these crimes? Will

American business men, whose legitimate business and investments have been blocked by German capitalists, cherish no resentment? Will American universities tolerate professors who have been slyly preaching sedition? It is far more likely that for a generation to come the very word "German" will be detested in the United States and that every German will have to show cause why he should not be regarded as a secret enemy of this country. The survivors and descendants of those who are now abetting the conspiracy against the United States in behalf of a foreign Power will be as eager as were the Copperheads after the Civil War to have their past forgotten. The hyphens will fall: the citizens of this country will be Americans and nothing else; there will be no mongrel citizenship to be used as a mask for treason. The plotters against the United States, and their accomplices, native or foreign, make the fatal mistake of supposing that Americans will long tolerate in the White House

a President who lacks courage. Courage and
Honesty are the two qualities which, in the
long run, they set most store by in their
Presidents. Tragic would be the occasion if
hostile critics identified Cowardice and Dishonesty.

CHAPTER XIII

THE SHIPWRECK OF KULTUR

Wherever Germany extends her sway, she *ruins* Culture.
NIETZSCHE, *Ecce Homo*, p. 38.

Culture and the State are antagonists: a "Culture-State" is merely a modern idea. The one lives upon the other, the one flourishes at the expense of the other. . . . In the history of European Culture the rise of the [German] Empire signifies, above all, a displacement of the centre of gravity. Everywhere people are already aware of this: in things that really matter — and these after all constitute Culture — the Germans are no longer worth considering.
The Twilight of the Idols, p. 54.

Every great crime against Culture for the last four centuries lies upon their [the German] conscience.
Ecce Homo, p. 124.

MAN started among the beasts in whose struggle for existence there is the unending play and counterplay between brute force and cunning. Man became Man by sloughing off the qualities which chain the Beast forever to the Beasts' level. Measuring by geological ages we see him emerge with incredible slowness from Beast-hood into Man-hood; and so up through Savagery and

Barbarism, till he stands erect on the lowest step of Civilization; and then he mounts, still with groping hesitation, with frequent pauses, and with actual backslidings, the ladder of Ideals. Gradually there dawn in him instincts, motives, which neither the Beast, the Savage, nor the Barbarian ever knows. These are the stuff through which he discovers that he has a soul, the august and awful inmate of his inmost self.

Thenceforward Man fares on his journey through life, a strange blend of animal and of spirit — the animal in him always on the alert to regain entire mastery, and the spirit, though often baffled and betrayed, ready to renew its divine mission. This antagonism runs through all human affairs; and when the earliest moralists looked beneath the surface of life and examined the fortunes and deeds of men, they discerned that this is a moral world in which the forces of good and the forces of evil — God and Devil — battle forever for control. Subsequent scrutiny has always reached the conclusion that the only permanent good is spiritual. Pride of intellect, beauty of form and face, the conquests of science over the material world, the triumphs of war-lords after great battles won and imperial territories annexed — these are not the true measure of Civilization. True Civilization is of the spirit, whose treasure the world can neither give nor take away. How irrelevant, how external and fleeting in the presence of Emerson is the uncounted lucre of Cecil Rhodes or of Rockefeller! With what scorn would Washington have repelled the suggestion that he should exchange places with Frederick the Great! With what irony would Lincoln have dismissed a proffered exchange with William II! To Washington and Lincoln the possibility of being degraded to the level of Frederick and of William would have been abhorrent.

So rapid has been Man's subjugation of Nature, and so astounding the inventions by which he has turned her laws into servants of

his own will, that it has come to be the fashion
to mistake these things for progress. We
even hear them blithely lauded as essentials
of Civilization. But Man, and not his tools,
makes Civilization, and its character will be
either animal or spiritual according to his
nature. Ability to shoot up in an express ele-
vator to the top of a fifty-story New York
sky-scraper, or to motor a hundred miles in
an hour, or to telephone across the continent,
or to send messages by wireless telegraph,
does not constitute Civilization. It took
Shakespeare two days to ride on horseback
from Stratford to London; has poetry out-
soared Shakespeare in these days when one
can be whirled from Stratford to London in
two hours?

Inventions and ideas also bless or curse
according to the spirit of their user. Hardly
had printing been discovered, to bring incalculable benefit to mankind, before the Devil
saw his profit in it, and he has kept the
presses of the world supplied with copy ever

since. The modern probing into Nature has already produced a state of mind in scientific investigators which awakens anxiety as to the source from which their knowledge springs. Many religions have had a foreboding that there dwells something at the heart of the world which should not be unveiled, some primordial terror which, like the Gorgon, blasts those who look upon it. To hide this from the common gaze, mysteries were devised which it was sacrilege to attempt to penetrate, and Faith, not Reason, was declared the door to the truth that saved.

Modern Science, inquisitive and resolute, undaunted and tireless, has drilled its shafts of investigation, and has applied its microscope and its test-tube throughout the domain of Matter: and it has found Matter, and more Matter and nothing but Matter, apparently directed by material laws. The dyer's hand is subdued to what it works in. Assuming that there is a spirit in Man, might not that spirit be slowly stifled, *materialized,* and finally extinguished by continuous devotion to Matter and material laws? Might it not even come to pass that the worship of these material laws which Science has evoked should undo Man, as Frankenstein was undone by the monster he created? What if the Germans — having drawn aside the veil from the last mystery — have seen that Moloch is the Prime Mover of the world?

We cannot call material laws merciless, because they proceed from that which feels nothing. So human laws devised by materialists may be logically unfeeling; and the rulers of a people who have accepted the revelation that Moloch is God will naturally develop a system patterned after Moloch's commands. Ponder this well. If the Prussian pagan creed is true, then Moloch is God: his orders are the shambles of battlefields; the sacrifices most acceptable to him are the victims of combat and massacre; the hymns he delights in are the shrieks of ravished women, the pitiful cries of terrified little children, the mingled groans and curses of wounded and dying soldiers. His high priests are those who lead the teeming millions to slaughter — Attila, and Tamerlane, and William II of Hohenzollern. This is the corner-stone of Kultur, this the infernal abyss into which Kultur has already dragged Germany and would drag mankind.

Ponder this well. No plea for a place in the sun can justify the cruelty and the cunning which its attaining involves. The pomp of many armies, all marching obedient to the command of Moloch's Vice-Regent, does not hide the butcher's errand on which they speed. The Religion of Valor is a thin disguise for brutality, in which Man at the touch of the Devil's wand is metamorphosed back into his Beast Original. Patriotism becomes the disguise under which the primal instincts of tiger and wolf riot unleashed. In Kultur's triumph Civilization dies.

Kultur is not designed to benefit any other race except the German. If it conquered, it would revive the feudal relation of lord and vassal, Germany being the lord and all other peoples being her vassals. Kultur, as we have seen at every point in this survey, permits all things to the Germans. Their religion, their sense of honor and of mercy, their respect for common men apply only to themselves. German truth ceases to be truth when it crosses the frontier. Gott, the German deity, is a tribal god, made in the image of the Germans who created him.

Shall we marvel most at the patience with which the Teutonic genius has reticulated such a system, or at the overweening conceit with which each Teuton regards himself with supreme satisfaction and Kultur as the perfect Civilization which must be nailed down and riveted over the rest of the world? And what shall we say of a nation which at this late day supposes that any one political system can be the best for all nations? If you view mankind as it is, divided into hundreds of varieties, each differing from the others in traditions, in geographical environment, and in moral and intellectual capacity, you will surely conclude that to attempt to stand-ardize them would be as fatuous as to wrap the earth in a uniform climate. Such fatu-ity is born in the brains of would-be world-conquerors.

The great and deep and holy things of life do not come by the sword. World-conquerors by Frightfulness may command lip-service; they may batten on the fruits of their vic-tim's labor: but they cannot command re-spect or friendship, loyalty or love. Of all the conquering races, the Prussian has thus far been the least fitted to conciliate the van-quished. After one hundred and forty years Polish Prussia, although it has suffered unin-termitted persecution, remains Polish in de-sires and hopes and still requires to be terri-fied. Forty-five years of Prussian hectoring in Alsace and Lorraine have not diminished by a hair's breadth the French spirit there. In their more recent colonial possessions the

Germans have not even pretended to wish to secure the good-will of their subjects, it being a dogma of Kultur that the dark-skinned races are in fact only animals, to be treated as such.

But above political and military systems, above tribal customs and standards conditioned by climate, are a few hallowed principles which sum up the ideals of civilized men, ideals which even the least civilized have acknowledged, and all have endeavored, according to their varying capacity, to serve. Justice is one of these principles; Freedom is another; Pity, another.

The State worshiped by the Germans as an abstraction "above Society" is indeed just as personal as was its medieval prototype. But in the Middle Ages, Church and State went together; and the Church, which was the organ of religion, exercised, in theory at least, authority over the State in those matters into which religion or morals entered. But mark well that in the system devised by Kultur, the State is omnipotent. Kultur recognizes neither morals nor religion apart from political considerations. The conscience of the Germans and their public and private acts are in the keeping of this godless abstraction. No wonder that poor old Haeckel shouts out his octogenarian rejoicing that the war has proved that God and immortality are absurd delusions, and that Kultur is the highest achievement of Man.

I quote from a private letter, written by an eminent physician with the British expedition in France to a distinguished American physician: —

With all my soul I believe that the ideal of pity is the noblest thing we have, and that its denial, which waves on every German flag, is the denial of all that the greatest men have striven for for centuries. I see in this war the colossal strife between the doctrine which I call good, and *der Geist der stets verneint*. You see I am almost borrowing the language of the Kaiser. I feel that the two enormous spirits that move this world are showing their weapons almost visibly, and that never was the garment of the

living world so thin over the gods that it con-
ceals.

I am not much elated by the thought. I have
little opinion of Providence as an ally. I am
surprised at the weakness that the Kaiser shows
for his pocket Deity. What we have to do in my
opinion we do ourselves, and our task is none
the lighter that we defend the right. But I am
hardened and set by the thing I believe. I and
my dear boy [1] talked of it much as I am talking
to you, for we were close friends, and we felt,
both of us, that we were fighting for the life of
England — yes, for the safety of France — yes,
for the sanctity of treaties — yes, but, behind
these secondary and comparatively material
issues, for something far deeper, far greater, for
something so great and deep that, if our efforts
fail, I pray God I may die before I see it.

Kultur, which shuts out Justice and Freedom and Pity, shuts out Chivalry also, which,
if it be not fundamental like these three,
is the fragrance of the higher Civilization.
Saladin, the Arab, had it, in his conflict with
the Crusaders. It was the ideal of every
worthy knight in Christendom; it is a second

[1] The son had recently been killed.

nature to every modern gentleman. Grant had it at Appomattox, when he bade the vanquished officers of the Confederacy to keep their side-arms, and spared them the slightest suggestion of humiliation. But Chivalry seems to have found no lodgment in Prussia. I recall no generous act of Frederick the Great, or of Bismarck when he imposed terms on fallen France. The Prussian is not satiated by the overthrow of his enemies; he must see them prostrate in the dust and plant his heavy foot upon their necks.

A nation accessible to Chivalry would neither have ordered the torpedoing of the passenger ship *Lusitania* filled with noncombatants, nor have gloated over the crime, holding great meetings for exultation and gathering the children of the Fatherland into theatres and churches to sing hallelujahs over the destruction of those twelve hundred innocent souls. I turn away from such barbaric rejoicings to the pictures of the sea strewn with the bodies of drowned babies and of

drowned mothers clasping their little ones
in their arms. Happy those little ones, who
could never grow up to have hearts like the
Germans, bereft alike of Chivalry and of
Pity! Happy, too, those mothers, who displayed in the swift, final test of life that
mother-love which neither Kaiser, Krupp, nor
Kultur can vanquish.

Where was Chivalry when Von Bissing, the
Prussian Governor of Belgium, ordered Edith
Cavell's execution? If she had been guilty of
the worst crimes imputed to her, she might
at least have been put to death with decency.
Instead of that, Von Bissing let only a few
hours intervene between her condemnation
and her being led out at two o'clock in the
morning to face the platoon of soldiers. No
respite allowed for reviewing the evidence; no
person except the prison chaplain permitted
to see her; no friend to take her last message;
all hurried, clandestine, ruthless, as if Von
Bissing feared that he might be deprived
of his victim; he, backed by the full power

of Germany; she, one woman alone in an impregnable cell, ringed about by a fortress with regiments to defend it. And when they had shot her, Von Bissing's agents, wishing to debase her memory, gave out to the papers that she had quailed and broken down and pleaded for mercy: but the prison chaplain told the truth. Such is Chivalry as practiced by William II's chosen officers.

Thus, wherever we test it, Kultur breaks down. It has created a nation which boasts itself superior to the common laws of humanity; a nation which asserts that Honor and Justice and Truth, that Pity and Chivalry and Self-sacrifice, have no meaning for it in its dealings with the whole world outside. It might as well assert that the law of gravity or the formulas of algebra applicable elsewhere ceased to operate on German soil. Kultur, proclaimed by the Germans as a system which will overspread the earth, is in reality not universal, but local, tribal, narrowing. No modern race except the Germans could have invented it; so only Germans can both use it and glory in its use. It is like the harness of steel and straps which a cripple has to wear: by practice he learns to move about in it with ease; but though he be a giant, he is none the less a cripple, and the steel and straps are none the less a harness.

"But what!" you ask; "has not Kultur produced the highest efficiency ever known to man? Has it not trained sixty millions to such mechanical skill and mental docility that at a signal from Berlin they all turn east and bow in unison, and at another signal they all turn west? Has not Kultur created an army so perfect that its units and individuals could hardly be more machine-like if they were actually cogs and bolts of iron? Has not Kultur resulted in a system of education which directs every German at every moment of his life from the day he enters the Kindergarten to the day when he becomes a doctor of philosophy? Has not Kultur applied science to industry and to commerce as well as to the most trifling daily needs? Has it not subjected religion and philosophy, poetry, history, and letters, to the microscope of criticism? Has any other system imposed an equally rigid discipline or been rewarded by an equally submissive obedience?"

To all these questions there is but one answer: Kultur has achieved this, and the achievement marks at once the glory and shipwreck of Kultur. The object of every beneficent teaching is to take even human clods and evoke the souls latent in them; Kultur takes Germans and reduces them to the state of soulless machines. Efficiency is of itself no more praiseworthy than is electricity. The vital consideration is, who applies it and for what purpose. If the object be evil, then the harm done is greater in proportion to the greater efficiency. The voltage of a lightning bolt which sets fire to a town might supply power to run a dozen factories. Granted that Kultur-made efficiency ranks first, has it been justified by its works? Are the system which plotted for the Atrocious War, and the efficiency which has conducted it, to be commended as the final crown of Civilization? Would you who read be proud of your scheme of life if it revealed you as cruel, dishonorable, lying, unchivalrous, and as an egomaniac who did not shrink at murder? Under the touchstone of Kultur collective Germany stands so revealed. Satan, who turns all material inventions to his own uses, and sucks out the souls of men in order that their bodies and their minds may serve him, is the Master of that Efficiency for Hate which Kultur has bred in Germany.

"We don't care how many nations hate us, so long as they fear us," said recently a leader of German opinion. In such words Kultur epitomizes its message to mankind; in such words posterity will write its epitaph.

Kultur has had many forerunners, differing in specific aim and in scale, but similar in character. The Spanish Inquisition, for instance, was in essence almost the exact counterpart of Kultur. It strove to compel absolute submission to itself as the agency "above Society," not of the Prussian Gott, but of a perversion of the Christian God. The Inquisition threw over Humanity, Justice, Mercy, and set up standards of its own, intended to promote only its own interests. To secure conformity and obedience, it imprisoned, harassed, terrorized, tortured, and destroyed its victims. Like Kultur, the Inquisition maintained a large corps of eavesdroppers and spies. Like Kultur, it taught a nation to accept without demur its declaration that it was engaged in the highest mission known to mankind. It did not, indeed, organize an army to wage bodily war against its enemies; it simply used, in case of need, the armed force of temporal rulers to carry out its commands. It both aspired to be and was a world-power, in so far as it was co-extensive with the Spanish Empire.

Millions of people accepted the teachings of the Inquisition and fell quite naturally into the inhuman state of mind which such teachings induce. Like many a German who would personally shrink from committing cruel acts, the Spaniards and the other races whom the Inquisition held in subjection came to gloat over collective cruelty. How many millions of holiday-makers, men, women, and children, went out from Seville to the Quemadero and witnessed with rejoicing the *autos-da-fé* of thirty-five thousand heretics whom the Inquisition burned there in the course of three centuries? The feelings of those Spanish spectators, as they beheld such human sacrifice offered up by the Inquisition to its deity, did not differ from those of the Aztecs who watched the blood sacrifices on their pyramid temples, or from those of the French Terrorists who attended the daily exercise of the guillotine, or from those of the Germans who shouted their hallelujahs at the slaughter of the innocents in the *Lusitania.*

Under whatever name Kultur operates, it tends downward. The individual who thinks himself a Superman is likely to end in a mad-house or on the gallows: the nation, despotic king, or hierarchy, which substitutes its own selfish interests for humanity, shuts itself out from humanity, becomes inhuman, revives and worships standards of the Beast, and heads straight for perdition.

CHAPTER XIV

DESPOTISM OR DEMOCRACY?

Those arguments that are made, that the inferior race are to be treated with as much allowance as they are capable of enjoying; that as much is to be done for them as their condition will allow, — what are these arguments? They are the arguments that kings have made for enslaving the people in all ages of the world. . . . All the arguments in favor of kingcraft were of this class; they always bestrode the necks of the people — not that they wanted to do it, but because the people were better off for being ridden. . . . Turn it whatever way you will, — whether it come from the mouth of a king, an excuse for enslaving the people of his country, or from the mouth of men of one race as a reason for enslaving the men of another race, — it is all the same old serpent.

LINCOLN, *Reply to Douglas*, Chicago, July 10, 1858.

ON July 3, 1866, when Prussia, by defeating Austria at Sadowa, became preponderant in Germany, the Champion of European Despotism in an irrepressible conflict with Democracy was designated. Had Prussia been beaten there, she might never have dominated Germany, especially if Bismarck had carried out his resolve to blow his brains out in case of defeat. The triumph of Prussia then and her overwhelming victory in 1870 made her the citadel of European Despotism. Her talent for organization, the feudal instinct innate in the Germans, the Hohenzollern ambition, the tenacity of the upper classes, the bureaucracy, and the genius of Bismarck, all worked together to perfect a despotic machine fitted not only to repel the invasion of Democracy but to conquer it.

Less than half a century ago Bismarck predicted that constitutional government would soon cease to exist in Europe. By a noteworthy coincidence Moltke said that the Germans would have to be ready for fifty years to defend Alsace and Lorraine — a hint that he had created an excuse for perpetuating Militarism in the German Empire. Bismarck so disliked having a republic for a neighbor that he even considered intriguing with the French Imperialists to restore Napoleon III to the throne; but as time went on he thought that the lack of centralization in a republic and the inability to act quickly and unitedly more than counterbalanced the possible harm that might come from the sight of a republic on the German frontier. Sure of his competence to bleed France white whenever he chose, he took malign pleasure in the blunders of the French Republic, holding them up as proofs of the inferiority of the republican form of government. Before 1870 free institutions were the ideal of many middle-class Germans, and of some aristocrats; but after 1870 the ideal of Freedom slowly faded away, and the fact of Despotism, thinly disguised at first, took its place. The German incapacity for self-government, openly proclaimed by their leaders, from Bismarck to Bernhardi, was shown by the readiness with which they allowed themselves to be paternalized.

The only element which did not willingly take its place in the autocratic system was the Socialist. Bismarck persecuted the Socialists, and yet they multiplied. The Kaiser declared that to him "the word Social Democrat is synonymous with enemy of Empire and Fatherland," and he handled them roughly; but still they grew. Nevertheless, they have had as yet no influence in checking Militarism or in spreading popular liberty, and they were as chaff before a hurricane when the Kaiser proclaimed his Atrocious War. Prussianized Germany stood unshaken as the champion of Despotism. Nothing could be more natural than that Austria-Hungary should have clung to her as a vassal to his suzerain; because the Austrian dynasty was as insatiate as the Prussian for autocratic rule, but had grown too senile to exercise it successfully. So, too, the Turkish Sultan recognized in the German Emperor a bird of kindred feather whose golden perch he gladly shared. Nor is it insignificant that William II has exerted an influence on the Holy See surpassing that of any other Protestant monarch: for the Roman Papacy, like the Holy Roman Empire, of which the German Empire regards itself as the heir, was the most remarkable of medieval products.

Aristocracies are everywhere solidaire. One noble does not need to tell another that their existence depends on maintaining the social and political system which upholds privilege and assigns the highest privileges to aristocrats. But not the upper classes alone, every class which has acquired vested rights or a preferred social position resists the modification of the system in which it lives. The Prussianized German Despotism has very cleverly arranged it so that the Ballins, Krupps, and scores of similar capitalists, who, if they were Americans, German critics would brand as vulgar plutocrats, are much-honored members of the social organism. Indeed, Junkers intermarry gladly with the plutocrats, and the Kaiser has always shown a preference for millionaires — condescensions which relieve them from any social disability. But the really vital fact to note is, that the Hohenzollern Autocrat has bound not only the Court, the official Church, and the Nobility, but also Capital to his cause. The lower classes alone have not been completely won over. So powerfully welded together are the forces of Despotism in Germany!

Democracy has no such organization. If the President of the United States or of France, if the King of England or of Italy were to brandish a sword and shout, "My will is the supreme law of the State; I hold the life and death of every inhabitant in the hollow of my hand!" the people of those countries would burst into a roar of laughter which would echo round the globe, and then they would appoint a commission *de lunatico inquirendo*. That the Germans have listened reverently to such pronouncements by their Kaiser, accepting them as proper and logical, indicates how far apart Despotism and Democracy stand, and how irreconcilable their doctrines are.

Once all governments were despotic. Then

a group or class acquired certain rights. Then the conception of individual liberty was slowly evolved. Every one possessed an irreducible minimum of selfhood, most precious to himself, which no power had the right to deprive him of. Out of this came republics of free men and the gradual extending of political freedom from class to class, until the lowest received it and true Democracy was reached.

The peoples through whom this democratizing process worked came to regard the ideal of Freedom, like that of Justice, as axiomatic: a slave no more requires to be persuaded that freedom is better than slavery than does a sick man that health is better than disease. The champions of Democracy were too certain that its truths are self-evident and will automatically work the conversion of every doubter as soon as he hears them. The fundamental need of Democracy is discipline, and that is all the more difficult to organize and apply in a society based on the cardinal principle that each of its members shall be hampered as little as possible by the State in his personal freedom.

We are so accustomed to bemoan the defects and failures of Democracy and to overlook its mighty achievement that we too readily swell the chorus of its enemies. The truth, however, that the American Republic should have progressed as far as it has towards Democracy is more stupendous than that Prussia should have transformed Germany into a Despotism of the highest Prussian type. In America we had to overcome the inherent obstacles raised by geography and clashing sectional interests, besides the difficulties which confront a great experiment, and then we have had to assimilate forty or fifty millions of foreign birth or foreign parentage, who came mostly from countries where Democracy was unknown, and where the proposition that men are created free was scoffed at. Prussia, on the contrary, found the Germans a homogeneous people, already

230 GERMANY vs. CIVILIZATION

moulded as to temperament and customs,
and abnormally responsive to discipline, who
changed with little sense of dislocation from
the treadmills of their particular States to
the Imperial treadmill whose pace was regu-
lated at Berlin.

Prussia also, let us not forget, did not trust
to the innate seduction of her doctrines to
convert her German neighbors. She relied
first on military coercion, the method repug-
nant to Liberal souls. "Anybody can govern
by martial law," said Cavour. Nor should we
forget that it is easier to work to perfection
a lower species of government than to run a
higher species even with mediocre results.
As Despotisms were early forms, so they have
remained lower forms. I doubt whether the
efficiency of the Hohenzollern Despotism is
relatively greater than that of Rameses the
Second. The chief difference which would
strike Rameses, if he visited Prussia today,
would be that, instead of multitudes of
avowed slaves, he would find that the hewers

of wood and drawers of water, although the Kaiser's will is absolute over them, thought and called themselves freemen; and on inquiring, he would be told that this is a subtle tribute to the very democratizing spirit against which German Despotism has fortified itself. It tries to hide its own nature under a new name, but poison is poison, whatever the label on the bottle.

So the fated conflict between Despotism and Democracy is joined. Despotism has organized as never before. Under the flimsy decoy of the State it has enticed all classes in Germany to trust their destiny in its hands. It has taught them, just as the Inquisition taught its millions, that it is their mission to impose Kultur on all peoples, exterminating those who resist. It has revamped the pagan religion of Valor, in which Odin is renamed Gott. It has its willing historians and philosophers and its obsequious moralists and professors; it has its Krupp.

Its antagonist, Democracy, has never been

organized against such a concrete enemy; but
the time has now come when the Democratic
nations must prove that they can, not only
defend themselves against Teutonic Despotism, with its Turkish accomplice, but can
put down and hold down the outlaws who
would destroy Civilization and set up Kultur
in its stead.

We Americans must not be lulled into inaction by the belief that this Titanic struggle
does not and cannot concern us. The Germans
make no secret of their calculation that, when
they have destroyed the British Empire,
only Russia and the United States will stand
between them and world-dominion. Russia
is so backward that they think it will require
two or three generations for her to become an
imminent danger; but they regard the United
States as an easy prey — the "damned Yankees," as one of their diplomats recently called
us, are "so simple." With Imperial Britain
and the British Navy shattered, they reckon
that a few years will suffice to give them

control over here. The Atlantic Ocean has ceased to be a protection against material assaults; and since about 1900 the United States have been infested by the agents of Kultur who say now openly, what only a little while ago they whispered in their secret burrows, that they are going to Germanize this country. They have found demagogues — "demagogues are the commonplace of history" — to work slyly in their behalf, and they have gathered into their service unsuspecting sentimentalists, visionaries who delude themselves into thinking that the Atrocious War can be stopped by uttering a few ladylike phrases and that the wounds of the ten million living victims of Kultur can be healed by a little sprinkling of rose-water.

But this Republic, reserved by Providence to be the land in which the children of all races should unite and prove that the higher Democracy is not an unrealizable dream, must not perish now by the asphyxiating gases of the German propagandists or by demagogues and deluded visionaries. Having been warned, we must be prepared, not merely because of the peril that our own lives and condition may run, but far more in order that we may hand on to posterity the holy principles of Democracy, which many generations of the noblest men and women toiled and bled and died to establish.

The Liberty which Democracy aspires to is not a fixed substance. It cannot be prescribed in uniform portions to all peoples alike. It is, rather, a state of mind, a spiritual influence, which transforms those who possess it. If it were to be suddenly given to the Germans in the same measure in which the English have had it for generations, it would probably craze them. If it should adopt the creed of Kultur and set out to force itself on the world, under penalty of slaying those who resisted, it would cease to be Liberty.

Do not be deceived. In this conflict there can be neither truce nor compromise. Do not suppose, you who shuddered to hear how

Kultur practiced Frightfulness in Belgium, that the same Frightfulness will not be unleashed here as soon as an army of Kultur gains a foothold on our shores. The Germans here who shouted their shameless "Hoch! Hoch!" over the sinking of the *Lusitania* will indulge in orgies of rejoicing if ever they see New York or Boston or Philadelphia blasted by Frightfulness. The most honored men of these cities will be taken as hostages, abused and murdered as if they were Belgian notables, and the women — let Belgium teach what will be their fate. For the Germans sneer at us as a pusillanimous people, easily terrorized, and they think that we neither can nor will defend ourselves.

Two years ago few Americans believed that the Kaiser and his Ring would ever start the world-war which they had long planned. It seemed too wild, if not too wicked; and it seemed incredible that sixty million Germans really accepted Kultur as their religion. But the crime was committed, and Kultur has thrown down its mask. Let no one hope, therefore, that higher ideals alone will save Civilization, or that it is unthinkable that in this twentieth century a system which reduces man and society to a machine, which revives the barbaric creed that war is the normal state of the human race, which preaches that it is the duty of the strong to persecute and exterminate the weak, can overcome the world. Four centuries ago the Spaniards, who according to their lights matched the modern Germans, took the ascendant in Europe and held it for fourscore years, and wherever they settled moral and intellectual blight ensued. Let us see to it that the Prussianized Germans are not allowed to spread a similar blight and to restore under new forms the barbarism of the Vandals and Huns.

Do you believe that every man by virtue of being a man has inalienable rights which no master should deprive him of? Do you believe that the condition of humanity into which we all are born creates ties which bind us all together, and warrants each of us in looking for certain common attributes like pity and the love of liberty in all our fellows? Or do you believe that a few are born to physical strength which entitles them to dominate and enslave the others with whom they acknowledge no bond nor kinship? "Mankind," said Prince Windisch-Gratz, that typical Teuton, "begins with Barons." Is Love or Hate the corner-stone of your religion and the inspirer of your conduct? In the crises of your life, when you turn for help to another, does your ideal lead you to expect to see his human features fade out and leave you face to face with a wolf or a tiger? That is the culmination of Kultur.

Those of us who believe in Civilization know that Liberty — the soul of Democracy — is the condition without which permanent, spiritual good can neither spring up nor thrive. In its deathless presence the Imperial lusts of the Hohenzollerns, like the empires of those who were greater than they, are seen in their true nature, material, mundane, mortal.

> "For He that worketh high and wise,
> Nor pauses in his plan,
> Will take the sun out of the skies,
> Ere Freedom out of man."

THE END

𝕮𝖍𝖊 𝕽𝖎𝖛𝖊𝖗𝖘𝖎𝖉𝖊 𝕻𝖗𝖊𝖘𝖘

CAMBRIDGE . MASSACHUSETTS

U . S . A